The Data Catalog

Sherlock Holmes Data Sleuthing for Analytics

Bonnie K. O'Neil

Lowell Fryman

Technics Publications

Published by:

2 Lindsley Road, Basking Ridge, NJ 07920 USA
https://www.TechnicsPub.com

Edited by Jessica McCurdy-Crooks, cover design by Lorena Molinari

First Printing 2020
© The MITRE Corporation and Lowell Fryman. ALL RIGHTS RESERVED.

ISBN, print ed.   9781634627870
ISBN, Kindle ed.   9781634627887
ISBN, ePub ed.   9781634627894
ISBN, PDF ed.   9781634627900

Library of Congress Control Number: 2020931206

Bonnie O'Neil:

To my wonderful husband, Perry, who supported me through this process of long hours on nights and weekends. Many thanks for your love and support.

Lowell Fryman:

To my wife, Elizabeth, who kept me focused and allowed me to ignore her for many evenings and weekends to work on this book. After 43 years of marriage, she still lets me have room to make my own mistakes and follow a fresh path. It is never enough time but love never fails to fill the gaps.

Acknowledgments

From Bonnie O'Neil

It takes a village to write a book—there is a long list of folks that enabled *The Data Catalog's* completion. Many thanks go to my MITRE colleagues who supplied lots of support.

Our reviewers put up with short deadlines and gave incredible feedback:

- Adrienne Chan-Young
- Sanjeev Chauhan
- Qiang Lin
- Rekha Nallappa
- Linda Peng
- Anandhi Sutti
- Sherri Walter

To some additional special people at MITRE:

- My department head, Betsi McGrath, who encouraged me throughout this process
- Anandhi Sutti, who worked with us several late nights, ensuring our story with Alation was right
- Shibasis Mitra, whose futuristic vision became a "midwife for our thoughts" and inspiration for Chapter 12—and who supplied the wonderful passage about Sherlock and Mycroft
- Savithri Devaraj and Mala Rajamani, who supplied a relationship diagram
- Lorraine Fellows, for her vast expertise in data governance and her graphics

- David Bloom, for an introduction to his terrific alternative analysis tool, CAATS
- Susan Schreiner, whose feature list was a great launching pad for us
- Harry Sleeper, Kristian Mulcahy, Ian Bacon, Mike Phelan, Anuja Verma, Kunal Sarkhel, Steve Ney, Curt Holden, Joseph Heidrich, Thomas Chrissley and Hamza Syed who contributed to the data catalog story at MITRE
- My project teammates, who put up with my sleepiness in meetings
- The MITRE legal department
- The MITRE Information Release Office

A huge 'Thank You' goes out to all the vendors who were responsive to my endless requests for information and screenshots, and who also worked with folks within their companies to ensure we received accurate information (and the permission to publish it):

- Virginia Giebel from Informatica, who was incredibly responsive and frequently answered questions in the evenings and weekends
- Alex Gorelik from Waterline Data, whose book gave me a new appreciation of Data Lakes (and lots of great ideas for this book's content)
- Eric Amster from Alation
- Nidhi Teerdhala and Connor Donovan from Collibra, who connected us with folks from Brussels
- John Stegeman from Waterline Data
- John McBride from IBM
- Michael Dee and Chad Smykay from Unifi Software

Thanks to Murali Kala, who helped me envision data governance in a very creative way and helped with an important graphic.

And last but definitely not least, to my co-author, colleague, and friend, Lowell Fryman, who is such a joy to work with. His insight at just the right time, getting me unstuck, and his wonderful gift of humor helped get us through the long editing sessions.

From Lowell Fryman

First, I would like to acknowledge Bonnie O'Neil for her contributions to the data management industry in the area of data quality and profiling, and now, data catalog. Bonnie was carrying the profiling torch and conducting classes when only a few technologies were available. Bonnie introduced me to the concepts and value of data profiling. More importantly, Bonnie has been a good friend for a few decades, ever since we shared a small one-person cubicle. Bonnie is the driver to create this book. Bonnie has worked many long days and weekends to put together the knowledge contained within this manuscript. Bonnie, thank you for allowing me to work with you on another adventure.

To W.H. (Bill) Inmon, the father of data warehousing, who has given much to the technology industry and cared about all the people who showed passion and desire to further the data industry. Bill, thanks for inspiring me and starting us on this quest to enable data to be viewed as an asset to the business. A data catalog takes us further on that journey. I wish you nothing but the best. May the wind always be at your back.

Thank you to my friends, peers, and clients that have provided me with so many challenges over the decades. I also want to acknowledge my friends at Collibra that I have worked with to extend our knowledge and usage of data governance and data catalog. Felix and Stan, keep it up and stick to the high ground as you always have.

Finally, to the many clients that have allowed me to assist them with their data analysis and reporting projects. May you recognize that the destination is important, but don't forget to smell the flowers along the journey. The journey must be fun.

Contents at a Glance

Contents

Preface

If you are reading this book, it is likely you understand that an organization's data should be managed at an enterprise level and that you hope to learn about some tools that can help you with that desired outcome. If that is the case, you have come to the right place.

At MITRE, we have been counseling government Chief Data Officers (CDOs) and senior data executives for years about the importance and value of data management. The Foundations for Evidence-based Policy Act (Evidence Act) of 2018 and associated Office of Management and Budget (OMB) guidance now stipulate that each Federal agency have a CDO; treat data as a strategic asset; maintain a comprehensive inventory of their data assets; create governance mechanisms and assess the maturity of their data management programs. With the release of these federal drivers, we have seen an increase in government interest in ways to manage enterprise data more efficiently.

If you are not a government CDO, but someone who works in the industry and is relied upon to make the most of your corporate data for increased profits, innovation and insights, you probably already know that improving how you accomplish this is a good thing.

Data scientists spend most of their time finding data and getting the data ready for analysis.[1] These vital human resources could be better utilized by asking questions and creating algorithms than by wrangling data. And worse, when applying machine learning techniques, a lack of knowledge about the data can lead to poor results.[2]

---

[1] https://hbr.org/2018/08/what-data-scientists-really-do-according-to-35-data-scientists.

[2] https://towardsdatascience.com/the-machine-learning-crisis-in-scientific-research-91e61691ae76.

In the past, I've spoken with University Affiliated Research Center's (UARCs) researchers to determine how to improve the sharing of research data. As a first step, researchers need a representative corpus for their training and test sets. In our interviews, the researchers stated that contextual metadata was usually insufficient to determine if available data is relevant to the research question without talking with the data owner or inspecting the data set directly. A catalog, when used consistently has the potential to improve contextual metadata, improve knowledge worker productivity, and improve overall data literacy by helping the data consumer decide if the data under review is fit for their intended use.

I want to thank the authors for the effort and care they took to write this timely book. It will help the reader refine their requirements, accelerate market surveys, and begin the formal acquisition decision process. I especially like the features list in Chapter 11, which helps the buyer see the breadth of what's available today. The features list alone, is reason enough to add this book to your reference library.

Betsi McGrath

The MITRE Corporation

Department Head, Data Management, Integration and Interoperability

Introduction

This book illustrates many of the features found in today's most popular Machine Learning (ML) data catalog products. Please consider that the market is constantly changing, new players are entering, and current vendors are releasing new features frequently. Therefore, the prospective buyer should use this book as a guide to provide a broad overview of the many features available, and perform due diligence, using the features list we provide in Chapter 11. Pay attention to graphical user interface (GUI) design issues such as layout and navigation, as well as scalability in terms of how the product will handle your current and anticipated data and metadata needs.

The best way to introduce data catalogs is to show actual examples of what the features look like, and not recommend one product over another. Products are selected to be showcased as good representatives of a particular feature set, not as the only product or even necessarily, the best product in each category. We also realize that "the best" product in any given category is also vulnerable to change due to market fluctuations and new entries. Of course, "best" is the one that fits your organization's use cases best.

We have relied greatly on vendors to provide not just screenshots but helpful diagrams and infographics. We let the vendors paint the picture, and we told the story, weaving together all the input from the various vendors to bring together the mosaic that makes up the many-faceted data catalog.

This book is organized into three sections:

- Section One, Chapters 1 and 2, presents the rationale for a data catalog and tells four stories of fictitious users and how they fare with and without a data catalog.

- Section Two, Chapters 3-10, presents the many different types of data catalogs, showcasing a few vendors representative of each.

- Section Three, Chapters 11 and 12, concludes the book by providing an exhaustive features' list and a summary of our adventures, ending with a futuristic look of where catalogs might venture.

The authors hope that this book will be a good survey of the data catalog marketplace and will help to make sense of the new and dynamic product offerings in this vital area. Data catalogs are required to make sense of an organization's ever-expanding, voluminous data so that it can be leveraged to assist the enterprise mission. The data catalog represents a monumental shift in empowering the data citizen in the quest of faster time to insight.

## CHAPTER 1

Introducing Data Catalogs

Organizations are drowning in data—it is overwhelming. The growth of data of all kinds is exponential, and surpassing an organization's ability to manage it, let alone exploit it. Data offers the promise of many benefits, from profits to efficiency, but in order to realize these benefits, it must be understood and managed.

Enter the Data Catalog, which is an automated inventory of data assets, augmented (powered) by machine learning (ML). An *asset* is a highly valuable resource that merits management. Assets include money, real estate, and personnel, all of which contribute to the organization's ability to perform its mission. Valuable assets must be tracked and managed. Data has universally been recognized in recent years as a valuable asset as well. It has great potential to maximize efficiency, pinpoint new opportunities, and report on the status of mission goals. However, as such, it requires management and tracking, just like other assets.

About data catalogs

A data catalog is an inventory of data assets that enables users to discover and explore all the data sources available, enhancing their understanding of these sources, enabling collaboration with other users to enrich the quality of the assets, and achieving more value from the organization's data.

A card catalog for data.

A data catalog is a reference for data very much like a card catalog works for library books. A card catalog helps readers select and locate the books that are potentially pertinent to a specific research endeavor. It provides lots of useful facts about books such as:

- Author's name(s)
- Topic
- Publication date
- Publisher
- Brief book description
- Dewey Decimal classification number indicating its shelf location

An "Amazon-like" online catalog for data shopping.

The shopping experience can also be another great analogy for the data catalog. Imagine you are looking for a new book from your favorite author, such as the one in Figure 1-1.

Figure 1-1. Browsing for a book

We are all familiar with Amazon's "recommender engine," which shows related items. Figure 1-2 shows what other customers buy together with your item.

Figure 1-2. Recommender: Frequently bought together

The online catalog shows what customers also view when looking at this item, as shown in Figure 1-3. This is helpful because you might spot one of the author's books that you might not have read.

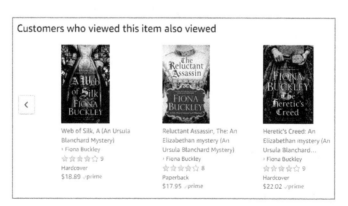

Figure 1-3. Recommender: Other items viewed

The editorial reviews along with product details and a favorability ranking are shown in Figure 1-4.

The online sales catalog shown in Figure 1-5 features a summary of the reviews based on five stars and actual customer reviews.

Figure 1-4. Book details and average customer review

Customer reviews
☆☆☆☆☆ 4.3 out of 5

5 customer ratings

5 customer reviews

Top Reviews ∨

Kindle Customer

☆☆☆☆☆ **Interesting read**
January 11, 2019
Format: Kindle Edition   Verified Purchase

I liked this book because Ursula wasn't constantly in mortal danger. Plus, it features my favorite Tudor character -- the Earl of Leicester.

One person found this helpful

Helpful   Comment   Report abuse

Review this product
Share your thoughts with other customers

Figure 1-5. Customer reviews

Data catalog features overview

A data catalog contains useful information about data assets of various kinds similar to the above examples. Some facts about data assets include:

- Name
- Description
- Topic or category
- Date it was loaded into the catalog
- Number of columns in a table

- Data format, such as relational database table, JSON, or XML
- Data owner or steward
- Location of the data
- Data set size such as the number of rows in a table or the size in megabytes (MB)
- Indication as to what the data looks like

In addition, data catalogs provide the common features we are used to seeing in online catalogs such as on Amazon.com:

- Related data assets
- Recommended data assets based on your searches
- Recommended data assets based on others' use of the data
- Collaboration features and crowdsourced features such as rating, comments, and blog posts

Some data catalogs even offer a "shopping cart" for data and an environment where data preparation and transformation can be performed.

This book will highlight many different flavors of data catalogs, and this section contains a preview of data catalog features.

Google-like search bar

Data catalog products have many user-friendly features influenced by Google and Amazon. For example, some catalog products feature an all-purpose Google-like search box, such as the one shown in Figure 1-6 from Unifi:[3]

---

[3] On December 17, 2019, Boomi announced their acquisition of Unifi Software. Boomi is a data integration platform vendor. It appears that Unifi will still be marketed as a standalone product for the near future.

Figure 1-6. All-purpose search bar

Data asset overview

Figure 1-7 shows an example from Alation on how a data catalog page provides an overview of a data asset. It presents the type of asset (the icon shows it as a database table), endorsements, Subject Matter Experts (SMEs) and data stewards, a text description—even the popularity of attributes in the table.

Figure 1-7. Data asset overview

Help and suggestions

Some data catalogs provide guidance in various forms when conducting searches, including Amazon-like recommendations ("people who viewed this item also viewed…"). Unifi provides a yellow lightbulb to the right of the search bar, which displays the language you can use to search for various data assets, as shown in Figure 1-8.

Figure 1-8. Search suggestions

Use of machine learning

Many data catalog tools use Machine Learning[4] (ML) to aid in recognition of tags and data types and assist in searching for data. ML can help the data catalog decipher what kind of data is contained in a field or column. Figure 1-9 from Waterline Data[5] shows four columns in a specific data set. Each column name reveals nothing about the data in the field, which may have been created by a random text string generator with no inherent meaning. Please see the first column name highlighted in Figure 1-9.

---

[4] "Machine Learning is an application of Artificial Intelligence (AI) that provides systems the ability to automatically learn and improve from experience without being explicitly programmed." From http://www.expertsystems.com.

[5] On January 22, 2020 Hitachi Vantara announced its intent to purchase Waterline Data. They intend on making it available both as a standalone product as well as integrated into its Lumada Data Services portfolio.

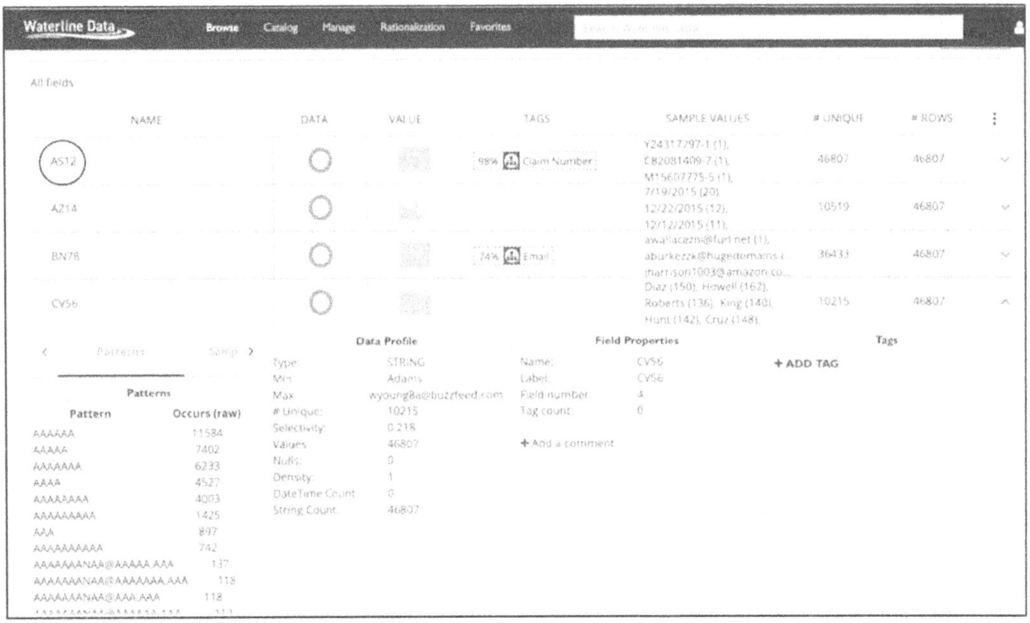

Figure 1-9. Machine learning recommends tags

Notice that the first field named AS12 is recognized by Waterline's recommender engine as consisting of a Claim Number, with 98% certainty. The dotted line around the tag means it is a system recommendation. The data steward can verify this assignment and click that it is true. Then, the tag will turn green with a solid line. ML can also greatly aid data governance and curation, pinpointing the existence of potential fields that may contain sensitive data.

Data profiling

Figure 1-9 shows sample values and data profiling results for each column, such as minimum value, maximum value, number of unique values, percent unique, number of null values, and even patterns and how frequently values occur. The profile results are shown underneath the relevant column, so the profile and pattern analysis in the figure is for CV56. Notice that CV56 contains mostly last names but the pattern analysis shows that CV56 contains quite a few email addresses as well. Notice also that the max value (in alphabetical sort order) is the email address wyoung8a@buzzfeed.com.

Diverse data formats

Data may exist in different formats, one of which is JavaScript Object Notation (JSON). Figures 1-10 and 1-11 show how Alation represents a JSON file. It depicts the schema, the actual JSON code, and the data in a tabular representation for readability. JSON is a nested structure, and as such, can be difficult to comprehend. The display depicted in Figures 1-10 and 1-11 can greatly help in visualizing the contents of the data. The screen is represented in two different figures for better visibility.

Figure 1-10. JSON screen part 1

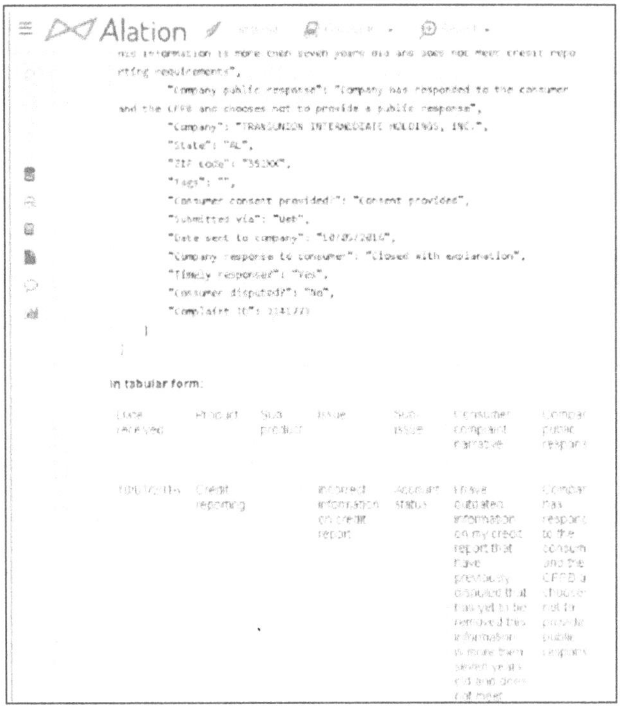

Figure 1-11. JSON screen part 2

Data lineage

Some data catalogs can capture the usage of data, such as seen in Figure 1-12. This lineage from Informatica shows data from several original sources moving to an MDM hub and finally to a warehouse customer mailing list. It would help data analysts to understand the pipeline of the data; where it was sourced, how it flows, and the transformations used.

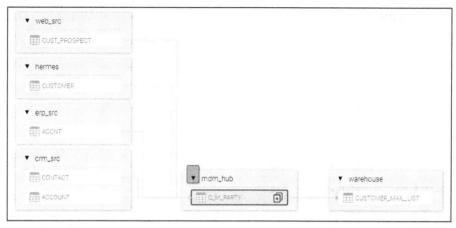

Figure 1-12. Data lineage

Collaboration and user ratings

Many catalog products allow users to rate data assets and provide comments about the data. Some products allow users to create tags. Figure 1-13 shows Waterline Data's rating feature in the "Reviews" section of the screen.

Figure 1-13. User review breakdown

Figure 1-14 shows Alation's conversations that analysts are having regarding a specific data set.

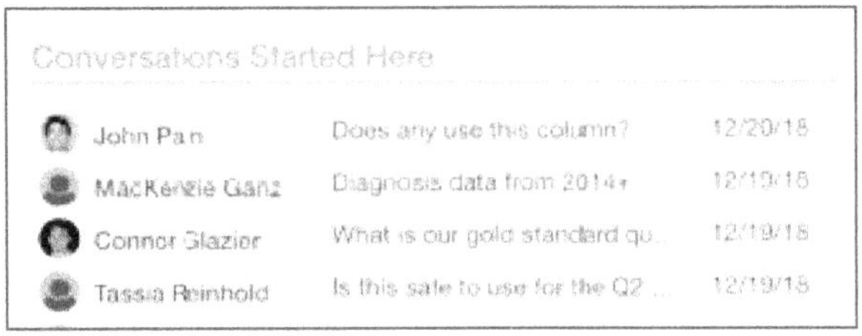

Figure 1-14. User conversations

Data catalog benefits

Most organizations produce a lot of data (and also ingest a lot of external data) but are unable to make any sense of their data. Furthermore, most organizations don't know what data they have and don't have. How can you manage and control what you don't know?

The search and curation benefits of a data catalog enable an organization to maximize its corporate knowledge in areas such as:

- e-discovery
- Legal matters
- Regulatory compliance
- Policy enforcement
- Privacy protection
- Risk management
- Security
- Data usage agreements (DUAs)
- Financial data rules
- New insights leading to higher profits or cost savings

Search

The most recognizable benefit of a data catalog is its search facility, adding context to data and therefore enhancing understanding for data analysts and data scientists. InfoWorld reported: "Most data scientists spend only 20 percent of their time on actual data analysis and 80 percent of their time finding, cleaning, and reorganizing huge amounts of data, which is an inefficient data strategy."[6]

Data scientists indeed spend most of their time looking for and trying to decipher which data sets are appropriate for their further study. Data set and column names are deceptive and often don't provide reliable information about the actual data that the name seems to indicate, as seen in Figure 1-9 above. What if the columns that appear to be the most promising are all NULL? NULL is equivalent to empty (no values) which could mean unknown. Data analysts also want to know who is using the data—did they find it useful for their purposes? What other studies are based on this data set and are they similar to the study I'm currently working on?

Data catalogs can be used to answer these questions. They provide rich **metadata**[7] which can aid analysts' understanding. They can provide a window into the contents of the data without the analyst having to perform many preliminary steps to investigate it themselves. Analysts generally have to prepare the data for analysis and clean it. However, a data catalog can help them locate versions of the data that have already been cleaned, saving them the

---

[6] "The 80/20 data science dilemma", InfoWorld, September 26, 2017. https://bit.ly/2RBcErh.

[7] The term "metadata" refers to data that describes other data. SharePoint prompts a user who is uploading a document to provide various information about that document, such as who the author is (it may be different than the person uploading it), its topic, etc. This information supplied by the user is metadata.

effort of performing redundant transformations. A catalog can also provide a forum for users to add their comments and ratings for data assets which can provide advice and pitfalls to avoid.

Management, governance and compliance, oh my!

Curation

Data catalogs also help simplify and reduce the time spent on the management of assets. Some data has sharing rules that must be followed when repurposing it or using it in a study. Some data may also be subject to regulations such as the General Data Protection Regulation (GDPR).[8]

The personnel role responsible for the management of data assets is called a **curator**. It is similar to a curator in a museum, who is in charge of the museum artifacts. Consequently, the task performed to manage the assets is called **curation**. Data governance will be covered in Chapter 5.

The data catalog contains the information where the data set resides in the Information Technology (IT) ecosystem of the enterprise so it can be found by both the analyst and the curator. Data catalogs help curators locate, manage, and track the status of data assets. For example, if an error occurs in a load or quality check, the curator can change the status of the asset to notify users of a potential problem, which may influence the analyst's decision whether to include that asset in a study.

Curation automation is very important, as anyone who has tried to keep track of data, files, or soft copies of reports knows. It solves problems such as:

---

[8] The General Data Protection Regulation governs data associated with individuals living in the European Union (EU).

- How do you know when there is a new data asset available?
- Were there changes to the data?
- When was the last time this data was refreshed?
- Who is using this data?

Manual inventories of data sets are usually maintained in spreadsheets or SharePoint. Both methods depend upon author initiative, adding a row in a spreadsheet manually or uploading a document in the SharePoint. The metadata captured is also not uniform and highly dependent upon the author's manual input. There is never any certainty that all relevant data assets are included in either inventory method. The location of the assets may change and therefore, search results are unpredictable and do not inspire confidence. Users and researchers, therefore, embark on their own manual search journey, scouring the intranet and internet looking for anything that might have potential. The net result is a huge waste of peoples' valuable time, which adds to the total elapsed time in which a mathematical model or report can be produced. The lack of confidence which stems from source ambiguity also casts doubt upon the final study's dependability.

Data catalog products can automate many ingestion and management tasks, cutting curation time down considerably, and helping to increase confidence in data. Curation can greatly benefit from automation, but a human curator can never be replaced by automation. For example, human curation is still required to make judgment calls on automated suggestions. The tool performs the rote tasks, allowing the user to focus on the more important tasks that require human judgment.

Key points

Curation and search have a synergistic relationship. Curation and good governance promote trust, and data engineers and analysts help curate by their participation and collaboration. Analysts contribute actively to the catalog, adding ratings and comments, which not only enrich the metadata in the catalog but in so doing increases the level of curation, as shown in Figure 1-15.

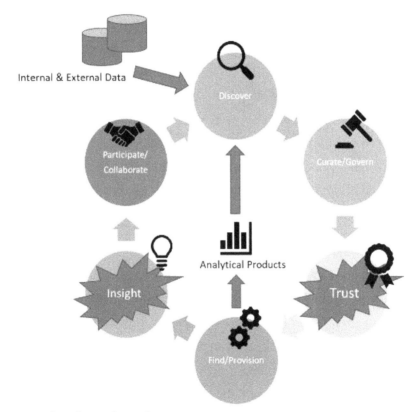

Figure 1-15. Curation and search synergy

Figure 1-15 shows the information and process flow of data asset usage facilitated by a data catalog. The discovery of internal and external data assets is governed/curated, which promotes trust in data use. The trusted assets can then be found and used in studies and reports which lead to business insights. Data engineers and analysts enrich the metadata by their ratings and collaboration, which in turn makes the data assets easier to discover. The data sets, dashboards, and statistical models produced by the provisioning process, in turn, are registered in the catalog as data assets also, which increases the corpus of discoverable assets.

A main benefit for curation is the ability to enhance automated data and metadata ingest. This is very important for "Data Lakes" or "Big Data" environments, see Chapter 6, Fishing in the Data Lake. The ability to add intelligent automation and metadata discovery to the ingest process is extremely beneficial. Data lakes often contain large volumes of data that do not have schemas that describe its format. Data catalogs can use automation and ML to discover the underlying format of the data.

Some data catalog products provide file comparison upon ingest and automated schema discovery. This helps both curation and search, facilitating understanding of the data by grouping files with like structure together. The ability to tie natural language names to columns further enhances the understanding of this data.

The ability of data scientists and analysts to produce meaningful, trustable data analysis products is in direct proportion to their level of data understanding. A data catalog is critical to the success of a business or government agency in order to promote data understanding. A data catalog provides many helpful features to enable search, discovery, management, and curation of data assets for the benefit of any enterprise.

## CHAPTER 2

A Data Worker's Dream

This chapter illustrates the need for a data catalog through sharing the stories of four data workers.

Data scientist

Megan has worked hard and has finally obtained her Ph.D. in statistics from a major university. This fine achievement has landed her an exciting new job as data scientist for a major health insurance company. Her first task is to determine what links may exist between certain allergies and environmental factors.

No data catalog

Megan's colleagues introduce her to the overall data landscape of the company. Their overview was brief and not very helpful. Where should she look to find the data she needs to study? Does it exist within the company? What about external data?

She finds that she doesn't have access to places where potential data sources may reside. She's not sure whom to ask, nor even if asking would gain her anything, because she's not sure if the sources contain useful information. She doesn't want to be seen as a pest, but where should she start?

She surfs the company intranet and after many dead ends, goes for help. After talking with a dozen other data scientists in the company, she finds one server that may contain useful information. She then locates the administrator of this server and requests access permission. She follows the procedures, fills out the necessary forms, gets her manager to sign, then gains access. She performs many queries against the data, and after finding that the most important fields for her research are completely empty, she sighs and begins the whole search all over again.

After several weeks of asking people, getting a little access here and there, and performing more queries, she finally finds two data sets that seem to be what she needs. However, on further analysis, she determines that the most pertinent data is in the wrong format—it will need to be transformed so she can perform her statistical modeling. She downloads the data, performs the transforms needed, and was finally able to conduct her study.

With a data catalog

James also lands a great job after obtaining his Ph.D. working for a similar health insurance company. He is provided with an orientation of the company's enterprise data catalog. His first study is to discover relationships between depression and geographic areas. He uses the data catalog to look for potential data sets to study. He looks for data sets first concerning the topic of depression. He finds quite a few. Scanning them, he sees that someone has already done a similar study!

This author of this study provided many helpful comments indicating which data sets were used as his sources, and advice concerning how he cleansed them and applied formatting rules. James performed a follow-up search on one of this study's sources and found that this source had not been updated in quite a while. There was a data steward listed, so he sent an email to this individual asking if there were plans to refresh the data. He also contacted the author of this study and asked for advice. Also, the data catalog had information about external data sources with geographic information he could download. He was able to gather all the information he needed in just a few days and was able to conduct his study. He published the study's metadata to the data catalog along with descriptive information so the next researcher would be able to benefit from his work.

Data scientist use case summary

These two stories highlight the difference a data catalog can make. The most visible difference is seen with cases similar to these, such as data scientists and data analysts who need to create studies, reports, and statistical models to assist the business in various ways. There are certain issues that using a data catalog can help mitigate:

- Data scientists spend most of their time looking for the right data to use

- Data scientists often publish data sets that are duplicates of data that already exist

- Data scientists often know where the issues are in the data and don't usually have a mechanism to communicate these flaws to others

- Data in most organizations is very distributed and as such are difficult to discover and locate

This is why a data catalog can serve as a Sherlock Holmes for data scientists. It can help them "sleuth" out where the needed data might reside. Sherlock Holmes was able to deduce all sorts of knowledge by following the facts that exist. The data catalog serves as a knowledge base that can be tapped to find exactly what a researcher needs to perform their study.

The data catalog that is equipped with Machine Learning (ML) will also be able to get smarter the more it is used. It "learns" about the environment, including the individual researcher and the searches he/she makes. The catalog can recommend data sets based on past searches and related data assets. It can also make inferences based on searches and assets added by similar researchers or similar topics. James can enter his topic "depression" and the catalog might also pull up data sets about similar topics such as bipolar disorder or mental illness.

Data administrator/curator

Is there a "data custodian" who keeps track of which data assets are where? Who oversees loading data into the organization's data ecosystem? Who monitors whether loads fail, and knows what to do when they do?

Data governance is the activity that is concerned with keeping track of data and ensuring it is fit for use. Chapter 5 focuses on a specific type of data catalog which serves as a data governance platform and also covers the importance of data governance. Similarly, data administration is concerned with monitoring, maintaining, and managing data. The role of a data administrator usually performs this task, separate from a database administrator, who is concerned with the upkeep of the database software. The data catalog introduces a new role called curator, whose job is to ensure that the data is properly loaded and to verify that the metadata is correctly captured by the catalog ingest process. Best practice dictates that the curator role is either split, with an IT person working in concert with a business steward, or with a business steward that is technically savvy. A curator usually takes on all the functions of a data administrator, plus the addition of monitoring the data catalog. The curator role must be performed in order to have the catalog function properly.

No data catalog

John is the data administrator of a large retailer. He struggles with keeping up with the influx of data coming into the environment, especially internet sales transactions and abandoned shopping carts. He also must deal with master data regarding products and customers, and reference data consisting of codes used in various forms. He struggles most with data scientists and analysts who are constantly asking for data and creating data assets themselves.

John considers his environment the "wild west" because there seem to be no controls around what is done with data. He published a SharePoint site where the data analysts and scientists can post their studies, but it mostly goes unused. He hears complaints that various databases have "bad data," but this is not defined—they fail to tell him how and why the data is bad. He has tried creating spreadsheets listing the databases in the organization but it seems an impossible task—sometimes the data is moved, new databases are created and he doesn't find out about them until months later. He publishes data dictionaries to help the data analysts, but these are also changed and the data modelers don't provide the updates.

With a data catalog

Mary works at a similar retailer. They are using a data catalog to maintain an inventory of the organization's data. Data ingests are handled by a scheduler, which polls the various regions where data resides. Mary monitors jobs closely, both to make sure that the ingest occurs properly, and there were no errors, either involving the data load or the metadata ingest. The scheduler monitors the areas where analysts and data scientists post their products. Data lineage is captured such that a data product that was derived from one or more sources is also recorded for data provenance. Data provenance refers to a record trail that accounts for the origin of a piece of data (in a database, document, or repository) together with an explanation of how and why it got to the present place.[9] Mary works closely with the business to ensure that the metadata that the catalog infers, such as auto-tagging, is correct. If an update job fails, she is automatically notified and she edits the catalog entry for that asset and indicates that it is deprecated, providing a cautionary note for analysts that may require the most current data.

One of the nicest things about Mary's job is that data scientists can browse the catalog themselves to look for data, so she doesn't have to field their requests. This frees her up to do the tasks she's most suited to do.

Data Administrator/curator use case summary

Data management and data architecture are very vast disciplines, composed of many sub-disciplines, such as data modeling, data quality, and master data management, to name a few. But at the heart of data management is being able to know what data you have so you can manage it properly. Data governance is about properly controlling an organization's data. As we have seen in Chapter 1, you must know what you have in order to manage it properly. Attempts over the years to manually perform data inventories have ended in failure and frustration, mainly due to data deluge. There is simply too much data to keep up with using manual methods such as spreadsheets or SharePoint.

---

[9] https://bit.ly/2v1cOza.

Metadata management is centered around the creation of a data inventory, along with descriptions about the data. The discipline of data architecture has long recognized over the years the importance of metadata management. Tools traditionally called metadata repositories have been on the market for decades. These tools have only dealt with the tip of the iceberg in trying to describe all the data. They have been mainly focused on technical metadata and have been highly dependent on manual efforts to populate the repository.

The differences that ML-augmented data catalogs bring for metadata management and data governance touch upon some major points that technology can finally deliver:

- Automated data and metadata ingest, including data asset discovery

- Data lineage and provenance that can be captured using automation

- ML inferences that can help populate metadata

- Automated alerts to data stewards

- Data governance workflows

- Semantic context through business glossaries linked to technical assets

- User-friendly interface for both searchers and curators

- Inferences for related data sets

- Users can assist curators by enriching metadata with their insights gained from using the data

Key points

This chapter has described how data scientists and data administrators would be positively impacted by the use of a data catalog. A data catalog can free up time for both types of users by facilitating the search for relevant data. The administrator/curator role benefits greatly from analyst users who can enhance and enrich metadata by relaying usage information to the catalog, which helps other users who are searching for similar data. Furthermore, analysts can trust the data more when they see that it has been actively curated, both by a data steward as well as by the feedback from other users. The links and semantic context added by the catalog are invaluable, and ML enables the catalog to grow "smarter" over time as it learns more from searches performed and crowdsourcing input from users.

The market is rich with many different types of data catalogs, each one providing different nuanced solutions. The next section will highlight these different types of catalogs.

## CHAPTER 3

The "Back Story"

Most data analysts and data scientists need to know the technical context of the data to figure out if a particular data set is useful, such as:

- What is the format of the data, such as database, file, or document?
- If formatted as a table or document, what columns are included and what are the data types of these columns?
- When was the data set created and last updated?
- How big is the data set? For example, how many rows are in the dataset if formatted as a table?
- Are the important fields all NULL?
- What does the data look like?

However, there's also the business content, the "back story," which is the story behind the data. The back story adds meaning and purpose to the data, such as:

- What do the fields mean?
- Is there a data dictionary for this data set? If yes, is it correct?
- Is there a business glossary that defines the terminology used in this data set? If yes, is it correct?
- Why was this data set created? What was its original purpose?
- Where did this data come from? What was its source?
- Who is using this data? Did these users find it valuable?
- Are there data quality issues in the data?
- Will I have to reformat, transform, or clean any of this data to fit my purpose?

- Are there any reports or other data sets that are based on this data? If so, are the reports accurate and/or useful?
- Has this data been certified? Can it be trusted?

Most data catalog products address many of these questions in one way or another. In this section, we will focus on the Back Story, the business context of the data.

About metadata

Together with Bill Inmon, we (Lowell and Bonnie) wrote *Business Metadata*. This book focused on metadata that businesspeople would be interested in, as opposed to technical metadata, which is designed to aid the database administrators and ETL programmers. The latter has been the focus of traditional metadata repositories for decades. Technical metadata is that data generated by IT products tracing all the technical information about the data. Examples of products that generate technical metadata include traditional databases, ETL (Extract, Transform, and Load) tools, data modeling tools, and BI (business intelligence) tools. Some examples of technical metadata are:

- Database table and column names
- Data types
- Data format
- Column length
- Column properties such as nullability (optional versus mandatory)
- Number of rows in a table
- Date of the last load
- Amount of time a load took to complete
- Load failures and errors

- ETL mappings and workflows
- ETL job status and logs

Business metadata is metadata that focuses on the business use of the data, such as:

- Definitions of fields
- Underlying meaning of the data and its business purpose
- Business use of the data
- Trustability/certification
- Business categories, glossaries, taxonomies
- Comments, observations, and annotations by users

Business metadata supplies the data's context, the back story.

The Internet is filled with examples of what is called "social computing," which means users rate, tag, and comment products, services, and places. Sites like Airbnb and Yelp feature ratings and comments as an important component. Users of these sites rely heavily on these crowdsourcing elements when deciding which businesses to patronize. Data catalogs that cater to the "business-friendly" aspect of data usage offer these same features. One such data catalog product is Alation.

Example: Alation

Home screen

The home screen shows helpful ideas for search, such as data sources, tables, and BI reports. Alation is also all about reuse, helping the analyst retrieve what they were last working on, and suggesting other resources that might be helpful. Figure 3-1 shows an analyst's home page. Notice the Revisit bar.

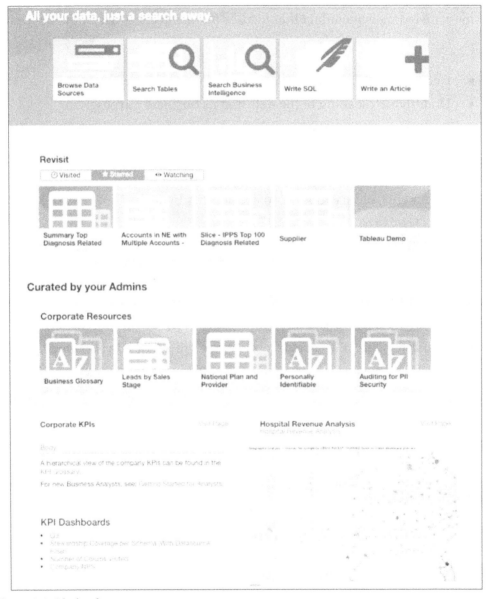

Figure 3-1. Alation home screen

The look and feel of the home screen are configurable by those users with the permissions to do so. Items such as a Tableau dashboard or map and Key Performance Indicators (KPIs) shown in the figure above can all be customized to make it convenient to use.

All-purpose Google-like search bar

Alation offers deep search of all types or classes of data in a very granular way, with a natural-language search capability. The user can type an English sentence or a fragment of an element name, and Alation will go to work. It brings back different types of data assets, including:

- BI reports such as Tableau or Qlik
- Values in reports
- Database tables, columns
- Business glossary terms

See Figure 3-2 showing a search for "people." This shows how Alation inferred that various assets may be related even though they didn't have "people" in the name, for example, "Number of Children." Alation knows that children are people too!

Figure 3-3 shows another search on "Health," bringing up an Industry Spotlight. The search brings up all sorts of asset types. Notice that you can narrow the search by indicating the type of data asset to fetch, such as tables, data sources, and schemas.

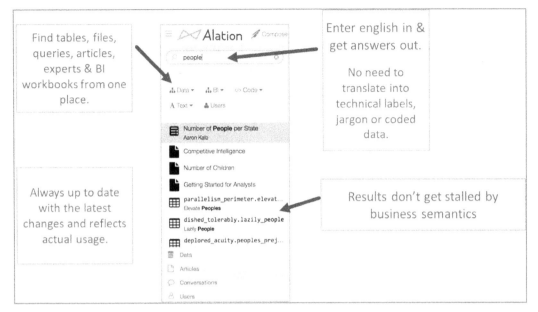

Figure 3-2. Search in Alation

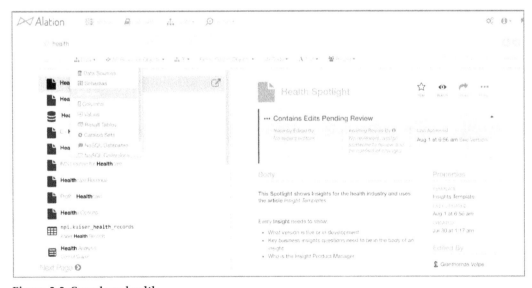

Figure 3-3. Search on health

Figure 3-4 shows an example of a typical catalog page for a data asset. This one is a table called sum_top_drg. The tabs enable additional content to be shown. The overview page shown is chock-full of helpful information, populated from contents of the business glossary. Notice that the screen shows the popularity of various columns. This can be very helpful, as it gives a clue to the analyst as to what others have found useful, and hence what might be useful for them. It also shows the top users. This provides a list of people the analyst can go to if they have questions about the data.

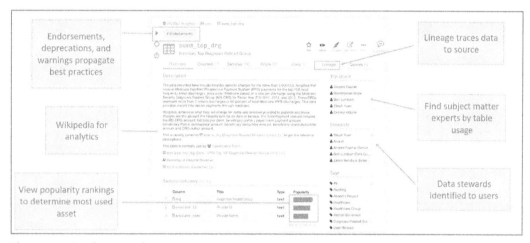

Figure 3-4. Catalog overview page

Text such as the description can be edited in a wiki-like fashion, bringing up an editing toolkit as shown in Figure 3-5. You can use rich text format or HTML format. You can add links to all sorts of data assets. Notice that there is an active link to something called "Tableau demo." Notice also that the data stewards' names can also be shown as links.

Figure 3-5. Wiki editing

Users can mark their favorites by clicking a yellow star at the top right of a data asset page. The star is circled in Figure 3-6. Notice that there are some other helpful tools such as "Watch." If there's a change to the asset, you will be notified. "Open With" allows you to go into another application such as a Business Intelligence tool like Tableau, or a database tool to look at a table.

Figure 3-6. Marking a favorite and a watch

Conversations

The feature called "Conversations" is a powerful chat tool enabling data analysts to "talk" to each other about data assets, asking for recommendations that would assist their analyses or gain context around the data usage of others.

In Figure 3-7 for example, the analyst is asking the data steward to remove an endorsement. Endorsements can be very helpful to guide analysts in the knowledge of data quality and join criteria. In this example, the endorsement of "last name" for a search or join criteria may lead to duplicates and inaccurate data. Notice that the contacted data steward was able to resolve the issue. "Resolved!" is shown in green.

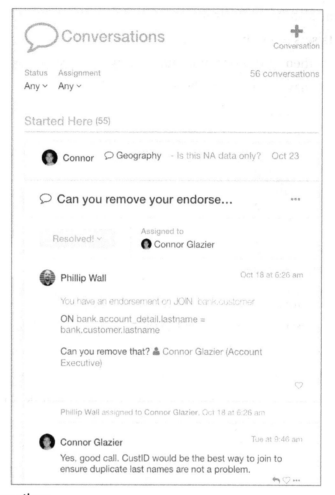

Figure 3-7. Conversations

An email server can be configured to help users contact a person that may not be active in Alation at the time of the request. The user can reference the username of another person beginning with an "at" sign (@), and if they are offline, Alation will send an email to the person alerting them that there is a conversation waiting for them in the data catalog. If they are online, Alation provides real-time chat facilities just like you would find in instant message applications.

An analyst can also browse through past conversations to get further insight into which data sets might be helpful, see Figure 3-8. This method can be used to get answers to their questions without having to directly ask the question themselves, as it may already have been asked. This is a great timesaver.

Figure 3-8. Browsing conversations

The method to create a link to another data asset's catalog page is very similar to referencing a username. You can use the 'at' sign (@) in front of the data asset's name when it is used in the text. This activates a link in the catalog so that the person can click on the name and it will direct you to that asset's catalog page. Alation replaces the '@' in the conversation text with a link, prefaced by the appropriate catalog object type; see Figure 3-9. Notice that the link in Figure 3-9 has a table icon in front of the name. You can also mark a conversation (as well as other assets) as a favorite, just like users can do in web browsers.

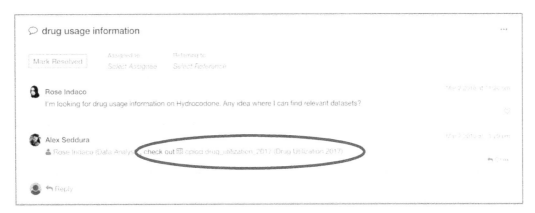

Figure 3-9. Links in conversations

Queries can also be referenced in a conversation with a link, see Figure 3-10.[10]

Figure 3-10. Link to a query in a conversation

Tags

Tags are a method of crowdsourcing, enabling users to create a means to categorize data themselves. Tagging allows users to create a "folksonomy," an alternative to a rigid taxonomy. The Techopedia definition of folksonomy is as follows:

Folksonomy *is the process of using digital content tags for categorization or annotation. It allows users to classify websites, pictures, documents and other forms of data so that content may be easily categorized and located by users. Folksonomy is also*

---

[10] Some of the figures in this book have real peoples' names so we have masked them to protect their identity. Other screenshots that do not have names masked are fictitious data and do not correspond to real people. (Or if they do it is not intentional.)

known as social tagging, collaborative tagging, social classification and social bookmarking.[11]

Figure 3-11 shows filtering tags by typing in text. Note that the list of tags shows the number of data assets referenced by that tag.

Figure 3-11. Tags

Tags are useful because they can be included in the search mix, helping to bring back more related assets, which ultimately makes things easier to find. Tags help uncover informally-related things.

Business glossary

Alation supports the existence of many sub-glossaries. For example, each division within an organization usually has its own terminology, which may or may not overlap with the terminology of others. You may have a situation

---

[11] https://www.techopedia.com/definition/30196/folksonomy.

where one division refers to the same fact with a different term than another. Alternatively, they may use the same term with different definitions.

Figure 3-12 shows a sub-glossary called "Banking" with multiple terms. The glossary itself (or grouping of terms) can have a definition (not supplied in Figure 3-12), and a template can be specified which guides the metadata to be included for each term. Additionally, a "table view" can be specified, which guides the display of multiple terms on the screen. A table view can be specified for a class of users, such as those who work in the banking department. A table view can be specified for all users as a default. The table view below shows a table with three types of metadata terms: title, author and content description.

Figure 3-12. Banking sub-glossary

A data steward can curate the terms and meanings as shown in Figure 3-13. The abbreviation "auth" is shown. Alation is recommending that it might mean "author." The little yellow robot icon signifies it as a recommendation, and no decision has been made yet. The steward can accept it (click the green checkmark) or reject it (click the red X). Notice that "authorizing" has already been accepted—the robot icon is green.

Figure 3-13. Term curation

Compose and recommendations

Alation has a "Compose" feature, which provides data self-service. It has benefits for both technical and less-technical staff in retrieving data for analysis. It helps less technical users write queries directly in the catalog, formatting accurate, syntactically correct SQL statements. It also cuts query test and debug time for technical users and provides a means for them to create "forms" for less technical users. Figure 3-14 shows the user typing "Dentists per State by Gender against Healthcare," and Compose created the query shown.

Figure 3-14. Compose smart suggest

The user types in "mal" and Alation's ML Smart Suggest utility shows some possibilities for this text string. Does the user want to filter on gender, perhaps, and "mal" is for "male"? Or might the "mal" represent a country that the provider practices in?

Compose's ML can figure out that when the user types "nor" in the context of a given query, it means "Northeast." In addition, it even knows which states are located in the Northeast. Figure 3-15 shows the recommendation of the states to filter on.

Figure 3-15. Smart suggest filters the states for northeast

Warnings will be displayed, which prevent improper joins and other possible errors. See Figure 3-16 and Figure 3-17. Relational databases can "join" tables together by means of a column in each table with similar data. The query below in Figure 3-16 is performing a join to retrieve the provider's state. Alation detects that there's a special table that has this information specially for medical records. Alation also catches that there are geographic filters missing in the query in Figure 3-17.

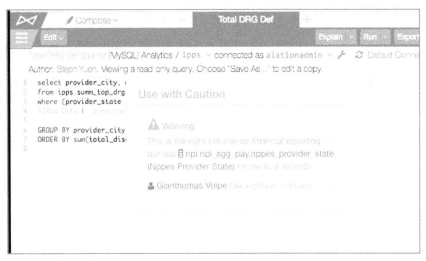

Figure 3-16. Warning in Compose

Figure 3-17. Warning regarding a query

Compose suggests columns in the data sets referenced and shows deprecated sources, see Figure 3-18.

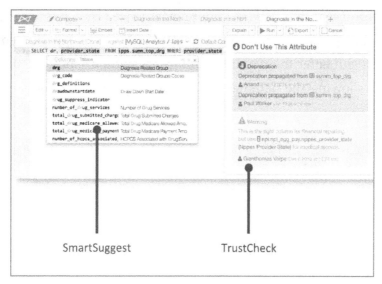

Figure 3-18. Smart suggest and deprecated data warning

You can copy or "clone" a query from somebody else—it will keep track of who is using your query. You will then get a notification that the query has been cloned by the user, along with their username. You can keep queries private to prevent cloning. Alation will show all sorts of query metadata, such as how many times the query was executed, when it was last visited, and by whom. See Figure 3-19. Note the "Cloned 58 times" message.

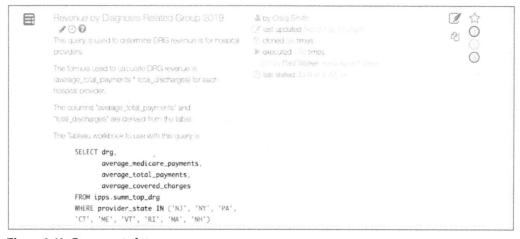

Figure 3-19. Query metadata

Another helpful feature involves a more experienced or power user creating a query and saving it as a form with parameters. The less experienced user can run the form and enter the required parameters without knowing the SQL. See Figure 3-20, showing the parameters that can be entered by a less experienced user.

Figure 3-20. Enter parameters

Privacy and protection: PII flags

Alation, like most data catalog tools, has various ways in which data administrators, stewards, and curators can protect the data. There are role-based security and permissions that can be set on many levels of granularity. An example of Permissions is shown in Figure 3-21.

Figure 3-21. Permissions

Data requiring special recognition and protection such as PII and PHI can retrieve warnings or flags, see Figure 3-22.

Figure 3-22. PII flag

You can mask columns, meaning that the column won't show up when sample content is shown, see Figure 3-23. The data in the column is masked with the word "SENSITIVE," so the data cannot be seen.

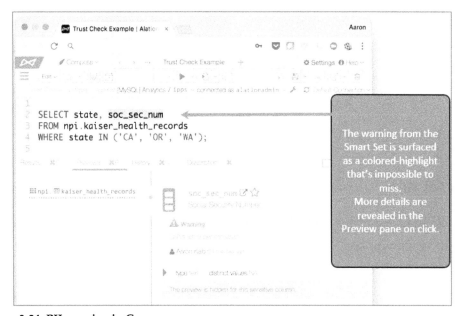

Figure 3-23. Masking sample data

Trust Check also comes into play when constructing a query in Compose, as shown in Figure 3-24. This figure shows the PII field highlighted in red with the warning. The user can click on the field and retrieve the details shown.

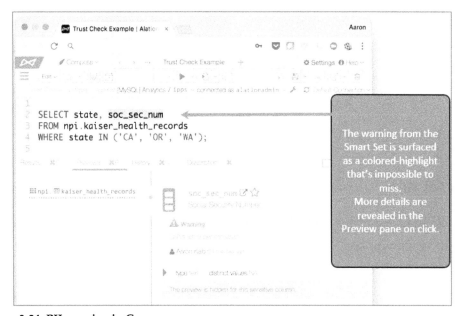

Figure 3-24. PII warning in Compose

Data lineage

Alation can display data lineage, as shown in Figure 3-25. The Hospital Revenue Analysis is indicated as a dashboard by the icon showing a meter. The Lineage diagram is accessed by clicking on the Lineage tab, which is underlined in orange. The diagram shows the table data sources traveling through intermediate landing locations to Tableau reports that are incorporated into the dashboard. The symbols in the diagram show the type of asset, such as table or report. Alation derives lineage from accessing query logs. The diagram below shows that a deprecated table is affecting the Hospital Revenue Analysis dashboard. Notice the red line. Data lineage is discussed more in Chapter 9.

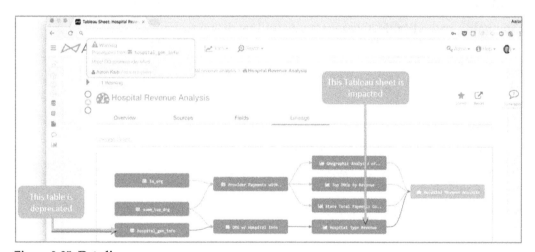

Figure 3-25. Data lineage

Permissions and roles

Alation allows for both a Server Administrator and a Catalog Administrator, but treats them as two separate roles, see Figure 3-26.

Figure 3-26. Administrator settings

Permissions can be set on all metadata and metadata types, and also for roles and individuals. Figure 3-27 shows Custom Fields, and the permissions for each, viewable and editable. Custom fields will be discussed next.

Custom Field	Viewable By	✏ Editable By
▦ Dictionary Provided	Everyone ✚ Add Rule	Everyone ✚ Add Rule
▦ Dictionary Analyzed	Everyone ✚ Add Rule	Everyone ✚ Add Rule
▦ Source Identified	Everyone ✚ Add Rule	Everyone ✚ Add Rule
( ) Instances	Everyone ✚ Add Rule	Everyone ✚ Add Rule
👥 Business Owners	Everyone ✚ Add Rule	Everyone ✚ Add Rule
👥 Stewards	Everyone ✚ Add Rule	Everyone ✚ Add Rule

Figure 3-27. Permissions

APIs

One of Alation's prime features is its ability to customize the data catalog, including displaying custom fields. This ability to customize is very powerful. It does this by way of APIs (Application Programming Interfaces). Figure 3-28 shows the addition of steward metadata for a data resource.

Figure 3-28. Custom Fields

Key points

This chapter presents many features that enable the "democratization of data" and empower data citizens of all skill levels who need data to get their jobs done. The range is large, from PhDs in statistics (data scientists) to business users to executives. Catalog products like Alation go a long way to open the possibilities to find, understand, and use data more efficiently and effectively.

CHAPTER 4

"Data Prep"

The early days of data warehousing involved business analysts performing Business Intelligence (BI) by using special interactive reporting tools. These tools ran against a data mart, a data structure especially created by using a "star schema" design for drill-down and rollup analysis across hierarchies. The data warehouse itself was also designed by integrating many different data sources using complex logic designed with Extract, Transform and Load (ETL) tools. The integration involved difficult matching rules to ensure that data was paired with semantically similar data from other databases. Data warehouses took months to design and build; consequently, they were difficult to change. It became very cumbersome to keep up with business changes in these monolithic structures. Data analysts felt like they were held hostage by the data warehouse. They wanted to respond to change quicker. They also would find new data sets and would want to integrate them with existing data in the warehouse.

Savvy business analysts and technical data scientists grew impatient with this system and wanted the ability to perform ETL themselves. Grassroots efforts emerged to "democratize" data and put more of it in the immediate hands of the analyst. Data preparation (often referred to as "data prep") tools are the result of this movement: The demand for data self-service.

Data prep not only involves the mapping and merging of diverse data sources but also transforming it into a common format and cleaning of data quality problems. This process is called *data wrangling*. Wikipedia defines it as follows:

Data wrangling, sometimes referred to as data munging, is the process of transforming and mapping data from one "raw" data form into another format with the intent of making it more appropriate and valuable for a variety of downstream purposes such as analytics.[12]

Data prep tools

Users of data preparation tools vary in technical acumen. Some tools are built to make the job of data engineering easier for those less technical, geared toward business analysts who may not be comfortable with the ins and outs of SQL.[13] It stands to reason, therefore, that the tools vary in degree of user-friendliness. All of these tools are geared to enable simplified matching, filtering, and transformation logic and ultimately the creation of analytical data sets. Data prep tools are essentially mini-ETL tools, performing the functions that previously were only done by the data warehouse development team.

Caution: The democratization of data empowers all data analysts with the ability to change the business rules on their own. This may have ramifications, especially if users do not communicate these business rules to others, or if their understanding of enterprise business rules differs from the rest of the organization.

The "Wisdom of Crowds Data Catalog Study"[14] by Dresner Advisory Services states that the "integration with self-service data prep tools" was the third top

---

[12] https://en.wikipedia.org/wiki/Data_wrangling.

[13] SQL stands for Structured Query Language, the language used to write queries in relational databases.

[14] Dresner Advisory Services, LLC. Data Catalog Study, Wisdom of Crowds Series. June 19, 2019.

data catalog priority feature, so it is, therefore, worth important consideration. Some data analysts appreciate the ability to "wrangle" the data right after they have found the desired data set in the catalog. It seems to be a natural pairing of functionalities.

However, some environments may have restrictions that prohibit data manipulation within the catalog, for instance, if data sets are governed by Data Use Agreements (DUAs), and every use must be scrutinized and sanctioned separately. Other data scientists may favor using their own environments and tools apart from the catalog. It is therefore important, when evaluating the need for a product, that pertinent use cases are well-understood before catalog products are evaluated. This chapter focuses on those use cases where democratization of data is important and the environment is set up to empower the data citizen to find and use data facilitated by the catalog.

One example of a data catalog with a user-friendly prep tool is Unifi Software from Boomi.

Example: Boomi Unifi

Unifi started out as a data prep product in 2014, helping to empower users and free them from the IT bottleneck. Then, data catalogs went "viral." Unifi had built into its product a lot of data catalog features to make democratization of data possible, with goals like "build once, use many" and collaboration. People using data prep tools need to be able to categorize their data sets to find them again and find related data.

Consequently, many of these tools have evolved some sort of cataloging function with ease of use as the goal. The Unifi catalog was naturally populated with metadata about the users' data prep tasks. The data catalog was therefore seen as an add-on to data prep.

Unifi decided to separate the catalog functionality and market it as a stand-alone product, in response to market demand. They have added many enterprise catalog features in order to do so, and can therefore be seen as a viable stand-alone product. However, its real power is realized when the catalog is paired with the data prep capability.

It should be noted that although some data prep vendors have added catalog functionality as an adjunct feature, many of these vendors' data catalog offerings are not really stand-alone enterprise products. Although Unifi has emerged from the data prep functionality, industry analysts[15] classify it as an enterprise catalog. Some catalog features are enhanced when the Platform (data prep) product is purchased with it. This chapter will, therefore, introduce some of these prep features along with regular catalog functionality, addressing the combined product offering.

Data analyst dashboard

Unifi has an extensive dashboard for the data analyst, shown below in Figure 4-1. This dashboard provides visibility into all the data prep tasks such as jobs, scheduled jobs, and workflows.

Note that this dashboard shows data sources, data sets, jobs, status of jobs, and so on. You can choose to see only objects you have created or those you have access to. Sometimes you may see the existence of an object to which you may

---

[15] Notably Forrester and Gartner. See bibliography for relevant research.

not have access and it is denoted with a lock. Permissions can be set, making these objects not visible to others.

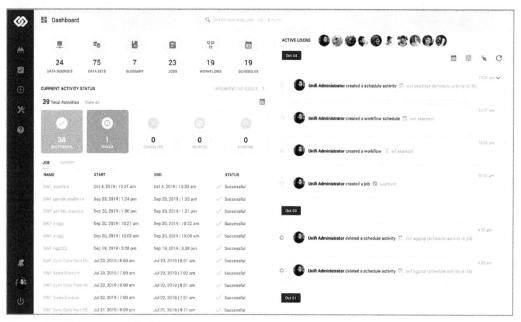

Figure 4-1. Data analyst dashboard

Dashboard functionality also shows active users and activity status, see Figure 4-2.

Unifi, like other tools of its type, allows for integration with Tableau. You can link your Tableau credentials within Unifi and then be able to click directly into a Tableau dashboard. See Figure 4-3 which illustrates all the various ways Unifi can integrate with BI tools.

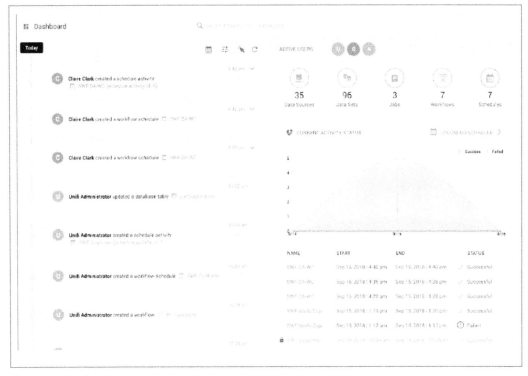

Figure 4-2. Active users

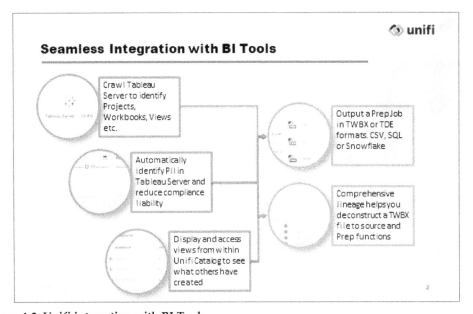

Figure 4-3. Unifi integration with BI Tools

Business-friendly search features

Unifi has many user-friendly features that less technical businesspeople appreciate when searching the catalog and choosing the data set(s) to use as input in a prep job. The all-purpose Google-like search bar is available on any screen. It can usually be seen at the very top of the screen. Users are presented with many helps to assist in finding the right data, as shown in Figure 4-4.

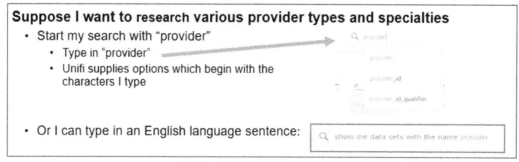

Figure 4-4. Search facilitation

Figure 4-4 shows how Unifi suggests ideas as the user types, bringing up items beginning with the search term the user has supplied. The user can also use a natural language sentence as Figure 4-4 shows. Unifi can provide several natural language searches as additional ideas when the user clicks on the lightbulb, shown in Figure 4-5.

Figure 4-5. Natural language search suggestions

Unifi also displays a "Recently Viewed" series of panes at the top of the screen, seen in Figure 4-6. The user can scroll to the right by using the arrow to see more recently viewed data sets. Notice the green indicator that the Customer data set is certified. (Note: the latest release uses a different but similar icon to represent certified.)

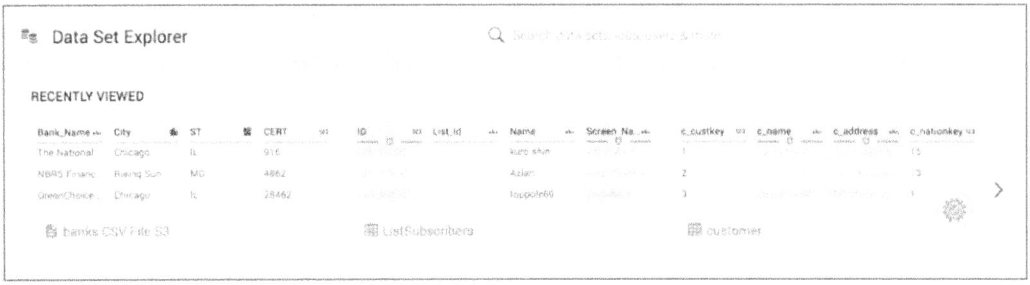

Figure 4-6. Recently viewed data sets

Unifi runs sampling and data profiling on every data set when ingesting metadata. The Platform product allows for profiling to be performed on the entire data set, but it is important that adequate system resources are configured. Sample data is very helpful and is shown whenever a data set is accessed (provided that the user has permission to see it). Sample data is available throughout the use of the tool and can be very helpful when composing jobs, as we will see later in this chapter.

Profiling statistics are shown along with sample data, see Figure 4-7, which shows a histogram depicting relative counts for values in the 'ST' field appearing to contain U.S. state codes.

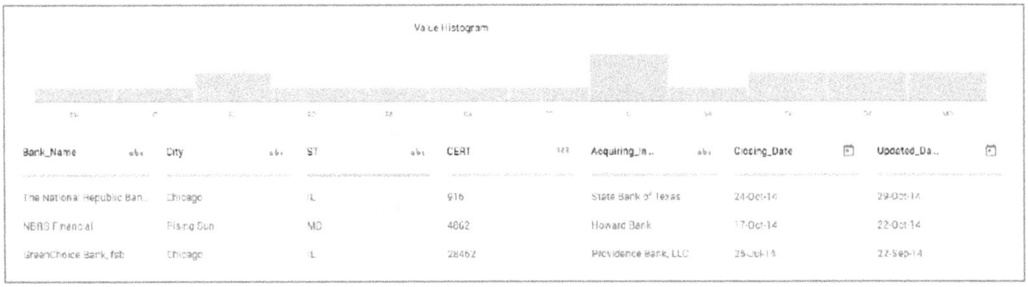

Figure 4-7. Histogram of state codes

The user can click on a histogram value to filter the rows by that value, see Figure 4-8, filtering by State='IL', all done visually. Notice that the CERT field is obscured. This indicates that the field merits special protection.

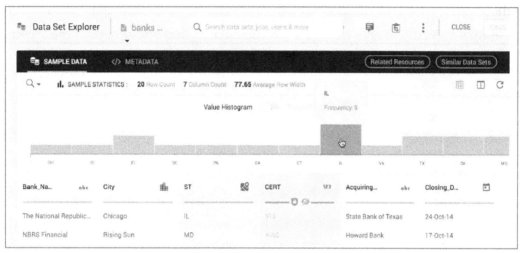

Figure 4-8. Filtering by using the histogram

Creating a prep job

There are seven steps to building a prep job:

1. Select data set
2. Join data sets
3. Enrich the data
4. Choose column
5. Add filter
6. Add aggregations
7. Output

Unifi makes it easy by walking the user through every step sequentially.

Step 1: Select data set

First, create a job defining its name, the type of job, and its description. Add any tags that might be relevant, and select the data set. Generally, you have searched the catalog first and decided which data set(s) to use. This step is shown in Figure 4-9. You will always start with one data set and add others in the second step. Notice that Unifi shows you where you are in the process.

Figure 4-9. Selecting a data set

Step 2: Join data sets

If you are only using one data set, you can skip this step. Unifi suggests data sets that can be joined to the one you have selected. These are shown in the OneClick Joins™ tab, shown in Figure 4-10. This can be a really big help to less technical users. Unifi will find the matching columns for you.

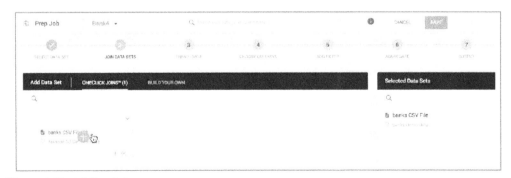

Figure 4-10. Adding joins

More experienced users can use the Build Your Own tab to select other data sets. This tab walks you through the join types, helping the technical user, as shown in Figure 4-11. You can edit the joins at any time. You can also see sample data that would be returned from the join.

Figure 4-11. Building your own join

Detailed metadata is available when building a job, as shown in Figure 4-12. You can also see sample data by clicking on the button at the bottom of the screen.

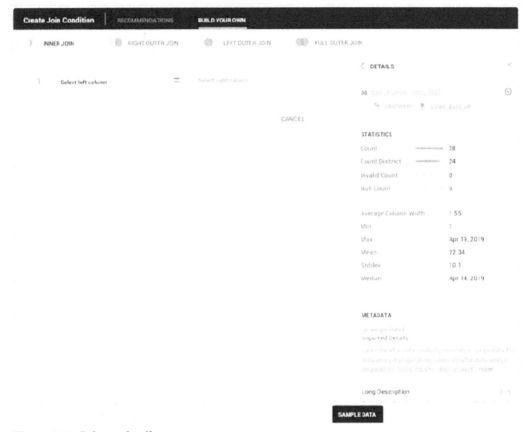

Figure 4-12. Column details

Step 3: Enrich the data

You can add functions that make the data set more understandable, such as the string concatenation of two fields, bringing the first name and last name together into one field. Common enrichment tasks also include adjusting the format of a field or converting it from meters to feet. Unifi has another useful feature to make the process easier like the OneClick Joins™. It has OneClick Functions™, which are derived attributes that have already been defined on the selected data set. See Figure 4-13 for an example.

Figure 4-13. Enrichment with OneClick functions

Editing the functions is also available, see Figure 4-14.

Create Function | ONECLICK FUNCTIONS™ (20) | **BUILD YOUR OWN**

BASIC   ADVANCED   DICTIONARY

Name
state_city   Description

Expression

concat ([banks csv file.Acquiring_Institution], [banks csv file.Bank_Name])

CANCEL   DONE   CLEAR

Figure 4-14. Editing a function

Editing can be done with assistance or advanced mode, and there's a dictionary available that displays the name of every function and its usage. Clicking on the function icon brings up the dictionary. They are sorted according to categories as shown in Figure 4-15. You can use Hive user-defined functions (UDFs) in Advanced mode.

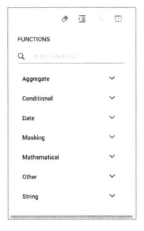

Figure 4-15. Function category list

Select a category by clicking on the down arrow. If you hover over one of the functions, you can click the "I" icon to show the details about that function. See Figure 4-16 for the definition and a sample showing how it works.

Figure 4-16. Function details

Step 4: Choose columns

This step involves picking the columns to appear in the output of the job. The columns are displayed according to the data set to which they belong. Simply click on the column names you would like to include. Note that if you have created a derived column, it will appear automatically and will not appear in the list to choose from. See Figure 4-17.

Figure 4-17. Selecting columns

You can see more details about the columns by clicking "View Selected Columns," as shown in Figure 4-18. Note that the expression is shown for the derived attribute. Sample data is available for viewing at every step of the way.

Figure 4-18. Column details

Step 5: Add filter

Next define a filter for the data set. Filters restrict the data set to only those rows which match the criteria defined in the filter. For example, you can use a filter like the one shown in Figure 4-8, by clicking on a value in the histogram (State='IL'), restricting the rows to only those customers who reside in the state of Illinois. Unifi provides OneClick Filters™, a list of saved filters that have been defined on any of the data sets and columns included in this job. They are shown in the Saved Filters area on the screen, as shown in Figure 4-19.

Figure 4-19. Adding filter

Step 6: Add aggregates

Aggregates are functions that allow you to provide summaries for groups of data. Typical aggregate functions are COUNT, AVERAGE, and SUM. You can group the data and provide a summary for each group or treat all the rows as one group, as shown in Figure 4-20.

Figure 4-20. Adding aggregates

Step 7: Output

The final step provides the user with the ability to reorder the columns. Unifi can format the output in a number of different ways, such as Tableau, CSV files, Hive, SQL tables or Snowflake. See Figure 4-21.

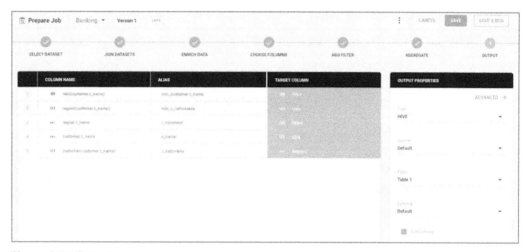

Figure 4-21. Output

Working with jobs

Summary tab

You can obtain information about jobs after they have been run. The Summary tab shows details about the last run, including the elapsed time and the time it took for each stage, how many data sets were used as input, and the number of errors. See Figure 4-22.

Figure 4-22. Job summary

Logs

Detailed logs are available and can provide help in troubleshooting jobs. See Figure 4-23.

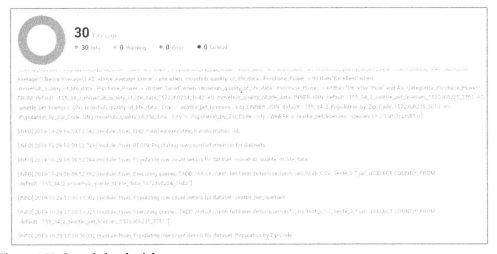

Figure 4-23. Sample log for jobs

Lineage

You can view the logs for a job, showing its history and status. You can also view lineage for the sources of the fields in the job, see Figure 4-24.

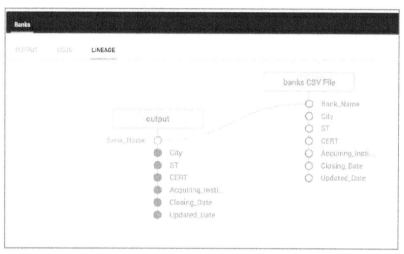

Figure 4-24. Job column lineage

Lineage can also show visibility into the function performed in a job, see Figure 4-25.

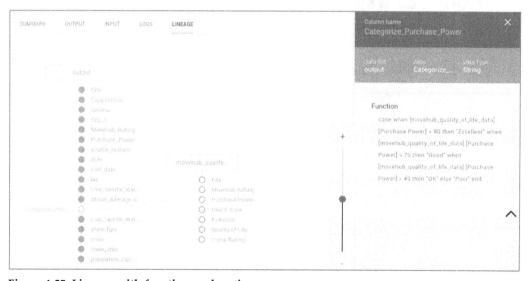

Figure 4-25. Lineage with function explanation

Cloning jobs

An important feature that Unifi provides is the ability to clone or copy jobs so that they can be reused. You can also modify jobs and make changes to any of the aspects such as the columns, derived attributes, or aggregates. History is preserved and a new numbered version is saved. The job screen is shown in Figure 4-26. One job is selected, and the Clone action is clicked. You would add metadata including a name, description, and tags if applicable.

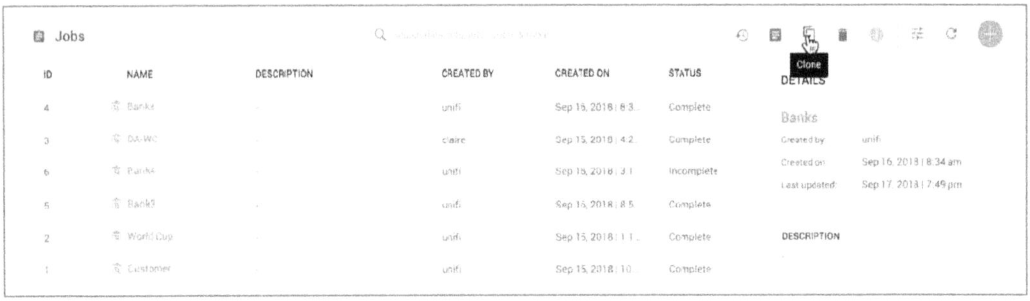

Figure 4-26. Cloning a job

Comparing data sets

It is very easy to create new data sets in Unifi—this is what analysts need to do. However, the proliferation of data sets can add complexity and confusion to the management of data.

Unifi provides the ability to compare data sets, which helps analysts determine which data sets are similar and which one is the best for their needs. When the user is viewing a data set, they can click on the icon at the top right called Similar Datasets and can use the weighting slide bars to determine how to judge similarity. The help feature denoted by the question mark provides instructions on how to use the weightings. Figure 4-27 shows data set name not weighted at all, and column name and datatype set to .5 each. Notice the warning at the bottom right.

Figure 4-27. Using slide bars for similarity weighting

The results of the similarity analysis are shown in Figure 4-28. Notice that Unifi finds potential duplicates, supersets, and subsets. Notice that the first two are flagged as Duplicates, the third and fifth as Supersets and the fourth as a Subset.

Figure 4-28. Results of similarity analysis

Clicking on an individual data set will show the statistics and the percentage of similarity (score). See Figure 4-29.

Figure 4-29. Similarity score

Ingesting and crawling

Automated ingest is an important feature for data catalogs and is accomplished in the Unifi Platform with its file crawler data source, which automatically creates metadata for all data sets as it traverses a given directory structure. The administrator creates a Crawler Data Source by indicating a Filesystem. See Figure 4-30.

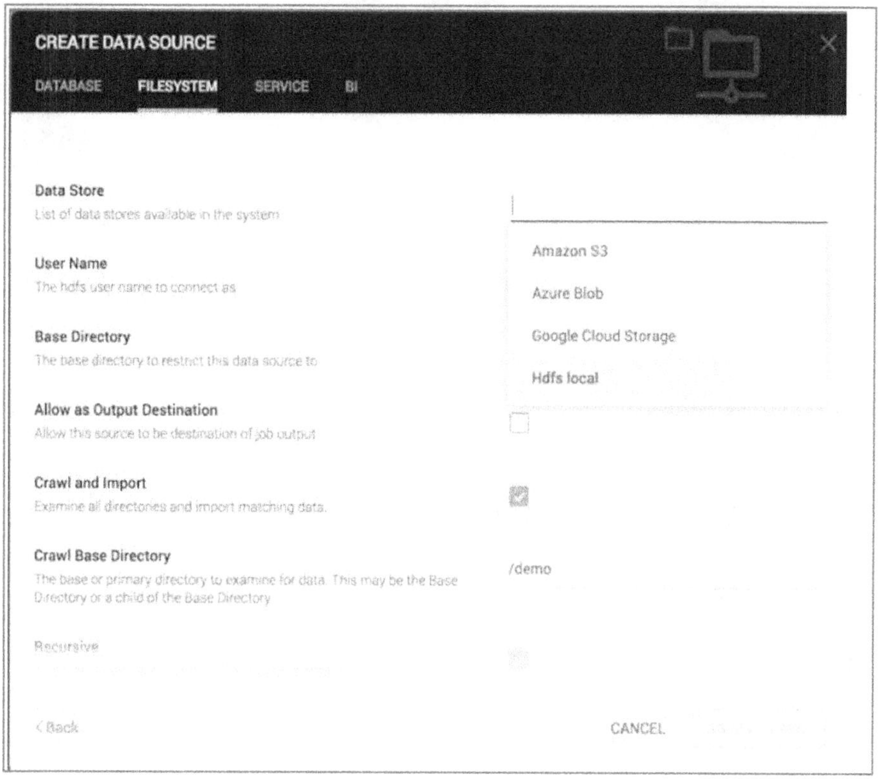

Figure 4-30. Create crawler data source

Certifying data sources

Like many data catalogs, Unifi has the ability for curators and others with appropriate permissions to certify and/or deprecate data sources, as shown in Figure 4-31. This is an important feature to have, especially when users are creating many data sets, and when many data sets are being ingested. Curation and data governance are covered more in the next chapter, Chapter 5.

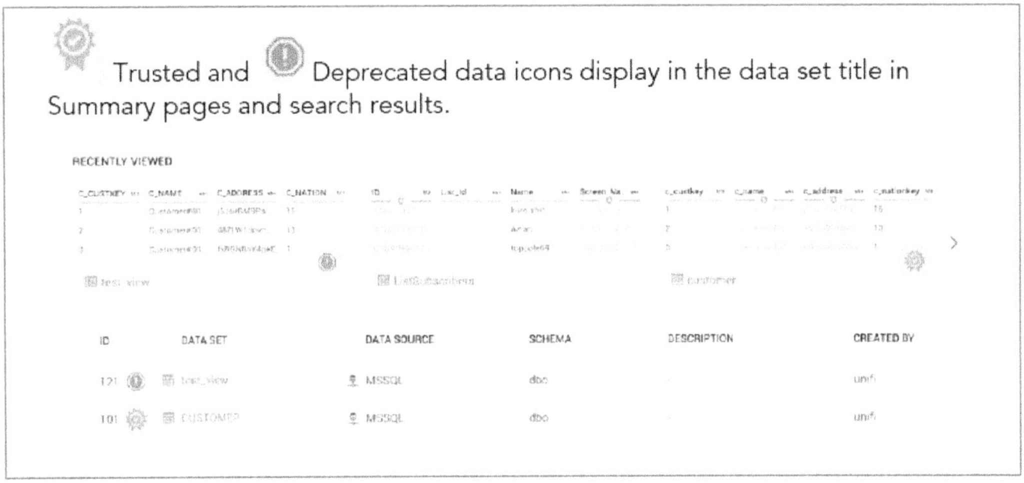

Figure 4-31. Trusted and deprecated sources

Key points

The availability of data prep tools within the data catalog itself can be seen by some data analysts and data scientists as a major convenience, critical component and companion to the data catalog functionality. This chapter has illustrated how data prep tools work within the data catalog and how they can empower the "data citizen" to not only look for data but put it to practical use.

CHAPTER 5

Data Catalog as a Data Governance Platform

Data governance plays an important role when deploying a data catalog. The data catalog possesses a complete or near complete inventory of data assets; therefore it is a natural progression to add governance functionality for those assets. Thus, every data catalog has data governance in its DNA.

Let's consider a little data governance history. Early data governance activities and software were focused on the roles of data stewards, which involve documenting definitions, business processes, primary business usages for analytics, and reporting of Key Performance Indicators (KPIs). Data governance became popular because compliance reporting became mandatory in many regulated industries such as financial services. Regulatory bodies began to demand proof that the reporting was based upon governed data. They required answers to the base questions of "what is this data, where did it come from and how accurate is it?" The data catalog, due to its bridging islands of information, can now be used to present trusted data to all data consumers.

The purpose of this chapter is not to be a primer on data governance, but instead to present how a data catalog can function as a governance platform and provide stewards with the additional tools they need to manage data properly.

Most organizations are overwhelmed with their data and find it difficult to produce a baseline data inventory, as we have discussed in previous chapters. The problems with managing data assets are well known and have existed for several decades.

It was hoped that data warehouses and business intelligence would make a difference, and they have. However, in many cases, the data warehouse has served as a spotlight for data quality problems. The lack of data governance to handle these problems has made most organizations aware that there are problems in the data, but at the same time, they are unaware of the data sharing complexity across the enterprise, and the difficulty of managing this data. BI users see data quality issues, like the tip of an iceberg, but underneath is the multiplicity of data mappings, conflicting sources, and inconsistently-applied business rules, as shown in Figure 5-1. The data catalog can expose all the complexity underneath the water, and data governance helps tame and manage that complexity.

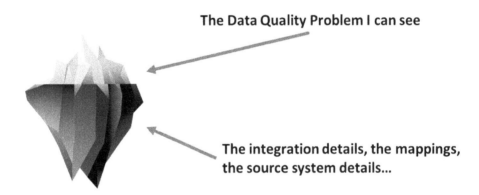

The Data Quality Problem I can see

The integration details, the mappings, the source system details...

Figure 5-1. Data quality problems are the tip of the iceberg

The data warehouse environment, however, did provide some data governance, which is why it took so long for data to be ingested and integrated. Data had to be semantically mapped to like data in other systems, which meant data modeling processes were done to understand the data, and then this data had to be brought together in a standard format and often transformed and cleansed. The process had to be repeated every time a new source was brought into the warehouse. However, even this painstaking process would not catch all issues, and users would invariably find them. It is often said that a data warehouse goes "legacy" as soon as it is released, because all of the initial work performing the mapping, cleansing, and governance processes would cease once the data was first ingested. In other words, many times these processes were not ongoing as the data warehouse evolved.

This means that even in a data warehouse, there is a certain amount of governance that goes on by the users themselves since nobody else is doing it. Users are often copying the data from the data warehouse, bringing it into an Excel spreadsheet, and running their own business rules against this data. This, of course, is dangerous. How do you know that the rules that the analyst makes up are in fact, consistent with the business as a whole?

Data self-service

The move toward "data self-service" and data democratization has made the "wild west" of analyst-created business rules even worse. Data is being brought into the enterprise from many different sources, many times by analysts themselves, and it is left up to them to figure out what the data means, usually without regard to the entire enterprise. The analyst usually detests this part of the job. Without a catalog to help them, they perform onerous activities figuring out what the data means and consequently map it to other data. They usually must perform many tasks in addition to this mapping and wrangling to prepare it for analysis. See Figure 5-2 from IBM and discussed in Chapter 2. This situation forces every analyst to do their own data governance in isolation, in a vacuum, and to create their own business rules. This is not a good scenario for the enterprise, because inconsistent and inaccurate data will result. Guaranteed.

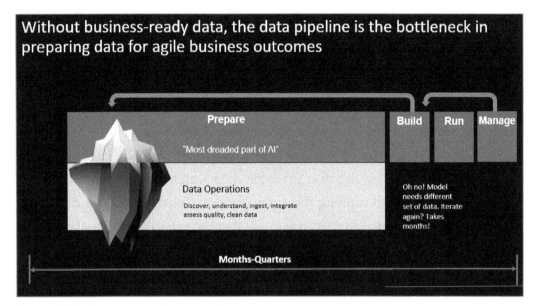

Figure 5-2. Data governance by the analysts

Solving the data governance problems across an enterprise generally requires an integrated data management approach for data and metadata. A data catalog can be the backbone of an integrated data management approach across the enterprise, supporting a diversity of formats, platforms, and types such as big data and data lakes. Non-integrated, stand-alone point solutions lack consistency and create a dearth of trust. The data catalog can be the unifying factor, a vehicle to make sense of data, protect it, and serve trusted data up to support an organization's mission.

Data curation

Data catalog curation must be performed in any catalog implementation.

> *Data catalog **curation** is the partnership of human interaction with an ML-augmented data catalog to make sense of, properly manage, and protect data.*

Here is how curation works: technical metadata is imported into the catalog. Business metadata can be added either manually or by import which defines data definitions, business glossary terms, data policies, and other artifacts that add business context to data; individual users can also add their own input such as tags. ML embedded in the catalog builds connections, bridging business context with technical data assets. The ML attempts to determine linkages between data assets and business metadata. The human helps to hone these relationships, accepting and rejecting their recommendations. The more the catalog is used and the business context is reinforced, the more the catalog "learns," and builds its knowledge base.

ML learning, in the beginning, is dependent upon user interaction, which approves and rejects the recommendations made by the catalog. Over time, ML will make better and better recommendations, requiring less and less human interaction—but the need for human interaction will never go away. This partnership between human and ML is discussed in greater detail in Chapter 6 on Data Lakes and again in Chapter 10 on ML.

Data governance

> *Data governance is the discipline of administering data and information assets across an organization through formal oversight of the people, processes, technologies and lines of business that influence data and information outcomes to drive business performance.*[16]

---

[16] J. Orr, <u>Data Governance for the Executive</u>. Senna Publishing, LLC, 2011.

Data governance involves the combination of policies, people, workflow, technology, and processes to produce data that is fit for use. Data catalog curation is necessary in order to launch an ML-augmented data catalog, but behind this curation, there must be a foundation of data governance in order to provide business-ready data. Business-ready data means that the data is fit for use by non-technical business people, without a lot of data prep.

Governance promotes understanding of the business context of the data across silos and across business units. It enhances data sharing by revealing usage constraints, ensuring data privacy and proper protection. It provides accountability for data quality and an escalation path to deal with issues, and in so doing it provides transparency, enabling impact analysis and data lineage tracking. It provides a means to manage and monitor risk. It can promote collaboration in the resolution of issues. And the data catalog can be a powerful enabler of all these functions, as we will see later in this chapter.

Data governance is, therefore, the process of ensuring the maximum use of data but, at the same time ensuring that the appropriate safeguards are in place. Another way to state this is to say that data governance facilitates the maximum use of data at the same time as it maximizes its protection. Balancing both needs is complex—you can't buy technology alone or take a pill to magically get both benefits. The goal is "Goldilocks Data Governance," see Figure 5-3.

 Heavy data protection often results in problematic data access, meaning users can't get to the data they need in a timely manner without a cumbersome process of access requests and multiple approvals. However, cavalier data access, allowing anyone and everyone access without appropriate controls often results in compliance violations and dire consequences. The goal is to achieve just the right balance of controls and access: "Goldilocks Data Governance."

Figure 5-3. Goldilocks data governance

Data governance facets

There are many facets in data governance and things to consider, encompassing People, Processes, and Technology. See Figure 5-4 from Collibra. The figure includes sub-disciplines and focus areas of data governance:

- Data Quality
- Master Data Management (MDM)
- Policies
- Risk Management
- Regulatory Compliance

Figure 5-4. Facets of data governance

Data governance includes these important tasks:

- Defining data and ensuring definitions are accurate
- Setting and enforcing data standards
- Derivation and metrics accuracy
- Authoritative data source certification
- Report verification and validation
- Data sharing rule conformance
- Data usage agreement control
- Setting and monitoring data controls
- Reference and master data governance
- Data integration and legacy replacement
- Access control
- Sensitive data and security/privacy control

These tasks are organized into main function areas as shown in Table 5-1.

Table 5-1. Data governance scope of concern

Data governance deals with virtually all aspects of data management.

Focus Areas	Examples of Data Governance Role
Data Quality	Defines and enforces quality policies/standards. Promotes collaboration to define DQ requirements and expectations. Prioritizes work to provide transparency into and improve critical DQ. Tracks issues, may also research, and either facilitate or manage resolution of issues.
Data Architecture	Defines and enforces policies/standards. Prioritizes work to understand the current data environment and collaborates to define authoritative sources. Promotes alignment with strategic goals of the business. Approves the future state vision.
Security & Privacy	Ensures through data stewards that data is categorized appropriately. Collaborates to ensure reasonably forseeable risks are identified and mitigated through controls.
Metadata Management	Defines and enforces policies/standards. Defines how data is collected, described and stored through-out all applications and databases. Prioritizes work to define existing data and to standardized metadata.
Business Intelligence & Reporting	Standardizes enterprise reporting (e.g. prioritizes migration to authoritative data sets, encourages use of conformed dimensions and shared data warehouse environments, etc.)
Risk Management	Establishes processes to identify and mitigate data risks in a business-driven context.

Some data by its very nature requires agreement from multiple people or divisions in order to be used properly. A perfect example of this is the creation of a metric that is used by management to measure some aspect of business performance. Figure 5-5 from Collibra shows a communication chain of 15 emails going back and forth to determine the definition of a metric for customer stratification.

One function of data governance is to set standards for metrics like this example. Later in this chapter we'll cover how the data catalog can facilitate this through workflows and collaboration.

Governance should also include oversight over Authoritative Data Sources (ADSs). An ADS is a data set that is deemed "official" or "certified." ADSs include Sources of Record (SORs) which are the point at which data is created — the point of origin. For example, a sales database may be the SOR for all customers in the organization. Customer data may then be extracted and loaded into a Master Data Management (MDM)[17] system, which may be considered an ADS, but the sales database, which is a SOR, is also by definition an ADS because it is the original source of the data. An important property of an SOR is that it is actively maintained. Other ADSs include integrated data repositories such as a data warehouse that is also governed and maintained.

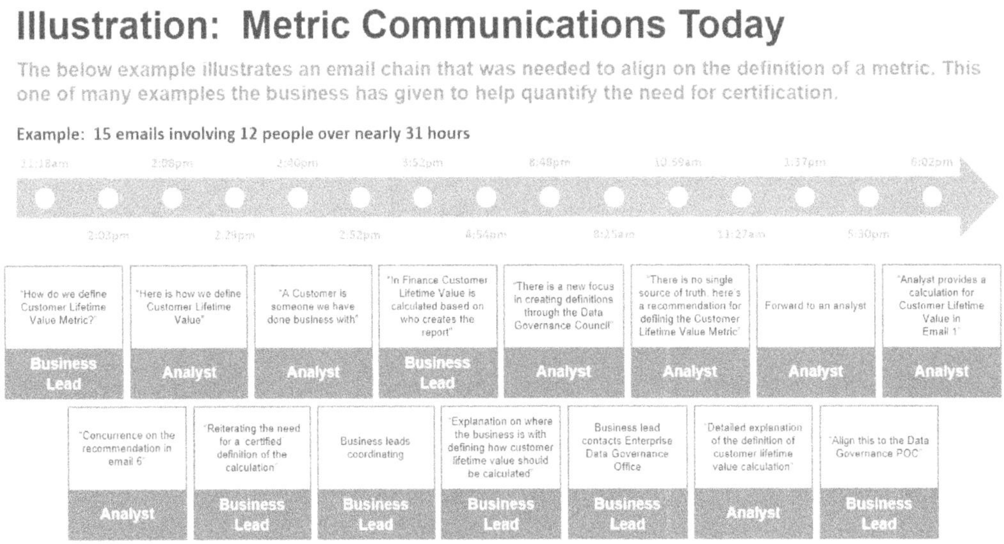

Illustration: Metric Communications Today

The below example illustrates an email chain that was needed to align on the definition of a metric. This one of many examples the business has given to help quantify the need for certification.

Example: 15 emails involving 12 people over nearly 31 hours

Figure 5-5. Email chain to define a metric

Data governance organization

Data governance takes some planning to set up the structure that is right for your organization. Typically for large organizations, there are several levels of governance bodies that perform different functions. Most formal data governance programs look like that shown in Figure 5-6. There's an Executive Level, a Management Level, Data Stewards, and Data Governance Operations.

---

[17] Master Data is defined and described later in this chapter.

Executive Level:
- Composed of an executive sponsor and members of senior management
- Decision makers who set the enterprise vision for data

Management Level:
- Composed of mid-level management
- Trusted advisors who frame options and provide recommendations for the executives
- Execute the enterprise vision

Data Stewards:
- Can be a variety of levels
- Responsible for day-to-day operations of business processes that create/maintain data
- Backbone of data management and governance

Data Governance Operations (DGO):
- Small group that supports each level of the data governance hierarchy

Figure 5-6. Typical formal data governance organization

This structure provides many benefits, most notably a well-defined escalation path for data issues.

A lighter weight, less formal structure includes data stewards to manage each major business domain as defined by the organization, often aligned with organizational divisions such as Finance and Sales/Marketing. This governance framework would be managed by a Data Governance Council and the Office of the Chief Data Officer (CDO). Figure 5-7 shows a data governance model with business Subject Matter Experts (SMEs) acting as data stewards in their respective organizations and evolving into a Governance Council. A SME is an informal role filled by someone who is extremely knowledgeable about the data. Notice that there is already a role in this organization called a "Business Partner" within these divisions. In the model shown, the SMEs and not the Business Partners are recruited to join the Governance Council. An alternative way to stand up data governance may be to recruit the Business Partners to be data stewards. A steering committee consisting of executives can be added as the data governance capability matures.

LIGHTWEIGHT DATA GOVERNANCE MODEL

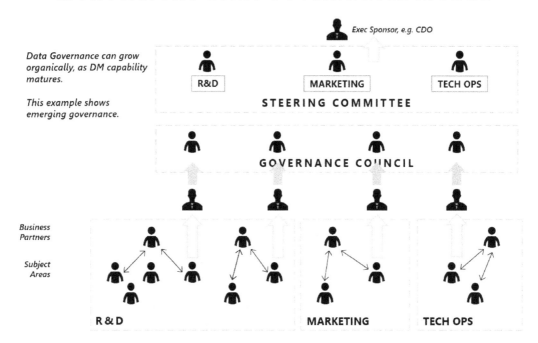

Figure 5-7. Lightweight data governance model

The critical element is that shared data is consistently understood and managed across subject areas and divisions within the organization.

Master and reference data governance

Not all data requires the same level of governance. Different uses of data and levels of integration across the enterprise will dictate different governance requirements. *Master Data* is an example of data that should be tightly governed.

> *Master data represents the business objects that contain the most valuable, agreed upon information shared across an organization.*[18]

Master data is distributed across the enterprise and used in operational processes and applications, as well as for analytics and business intelligence. Examples of master data include Customer and Product. The management of master data is aptly named Master Data Management (MDM).

This category of data should be managed by a data steward team, collaborating to ensure that the master data is kept up to date and used consistently across the enterprise. Often the type of master data will have a data steward who is the point person for that business domain (for example, Customer might be managed by the sales data steward) and his/her responsibility will be to manage it in conjunction with all other data stewards whose domains interact with Customer data.

Redundant data that is not managed exists in many diverse applications. These multiple copies of ungoverned data have long been a problem. Data analysts are often faced with the question, "Which version of this data is correct to use for my analysis?" Address resolution is a common example of this problem, where two (or more) applications have different addresses for the same customer. Which is the right one? This situation highlights the need for Enterprise Data.

> ***Enterprise Data*** *is defined as data that is used in more than one business area within the organization.*

Figure 5-8 shows the various levels of appropriate governance for enterprise data.

---

18 en.wikipedia.org/wiki/Master_data.

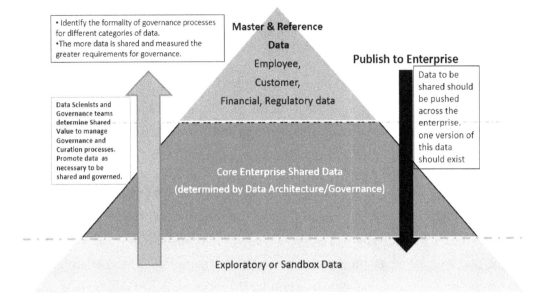

Figure 5-8. Levels of governance

Data governance often is involved with approving access to data. This is discussed later in this chapter, as we look at how the data catalog can enable data governance.

Data catalog role in data governance

Curation and data governance go hand-in-hand. The data catalog becomes the vehicle/instrument to assist with the appropriate usage of data. These usage constraints need to be built into the data catalog, which communicate any business, privacy, or security constraints that apply to the data. Just because a user is granted access to data does not mean that they have unrestrained usage. Thus, it is necessary for the data catalog to maintain knowledge of the data-sharing agreement that may exist and makes it accessible to users. Sometimes a workflow for requesting and gaining access to data is helpful and many catalogs have this option.

The data catalog is the perfect platform to facilitate data governance. It contains the inventory of all data assets and can be used to expose these assets so that appropriate usage rules and business context can be applied to the data. One such data catalog product specializing in data governance is Collibra.

Example: Collibra

Collibra has fully functioning data governance capabilities, including a Policy Manager and a Data Helpdesk. Collibra presents dashboards to the data steward when he/she logs into the tool. Roles and "Communities" are configurable. Figure 5-9 shows Collibra's Data Steward Dashboard, providing a birds-eye view into the steward's topics of interest, including counts of various asset types under the steward's management and pending tasks.

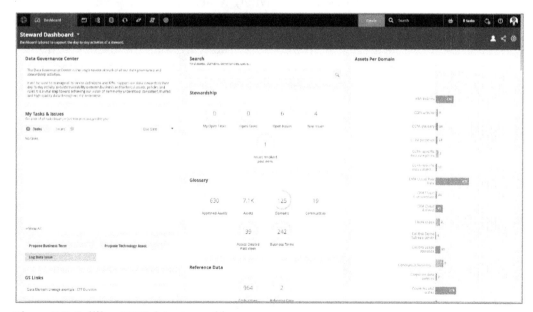

Figure 5-9. Collibra DGC data steward home

Figure 5-10 shows an example of a summary data asset page in Collibra.

Figure 5-10. Collibra summary data asset page

Notice that Figure 5-10 shows a data owner, which may be the same as a data steward (you can customize these roles) and a different name listed as a SME. Such a person can be a great help to the data steward and the user community and can field questions about the data, freeing up the data steward to perform other duties. Figure 5-11 shows Responsibilities tied to various roles. You can set the permissions for an asset-based role, a specific person, or everyone (all users).

Figure 5-11. Responsibilities/roles

The steward can navigate through more detailed information in the Data Asset page (Figure 5-10) by using the menu in the left panel. One of these options is

Diagrams, and one of the diagrams available is a Guided Stewardship Lineage, shown in Figure 5-12.

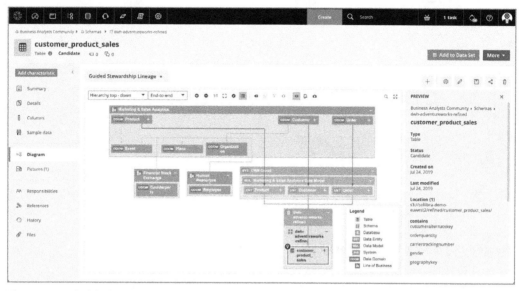

Figure 5-12. Guided stewardship lineage

This diagram shows how physical assets shown in orange and yellow are connected to business domains, shown in blue. Data lineage is discussed in more detail in Chapter 9.

Data quality

Data governance usually involves setting the standards for data quality for a governed data asset and monitoring its quality over time. The data catalog provides tools to do this and exposes the quality status of assets to users so they can see its quality before they choose to use it for their study.

The steward can set certain standards for data quality and create rules to measure it. See Figure 5-13.

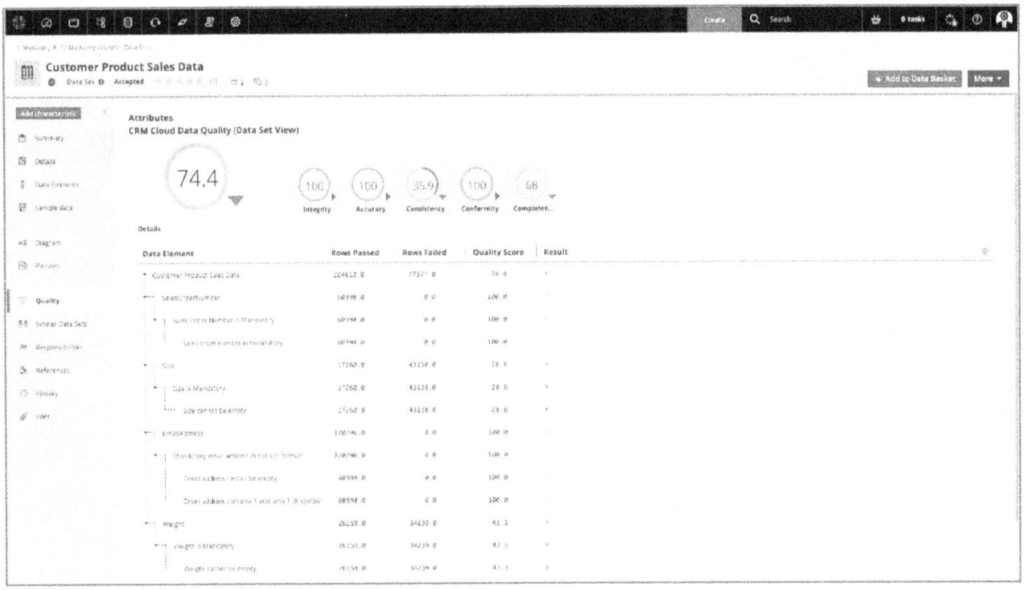

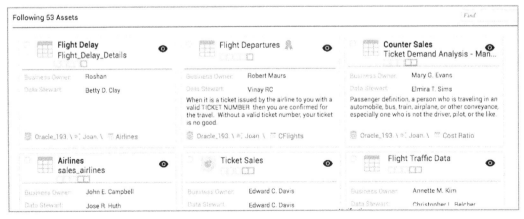

Figure 5-13. Data quality for an asset

The steward can keep track of all assets under his/her management by following the asset. However, analysts may also want to follow the data assets they are working with and get notified when new activity occurs. The assets that a user is following are called "watched" assets. Figure 5-14 shows a screen from Informatica displaying the watched data assets a user is following:

Figure 5-14. Watched data assets

Figure 5-15 shows the notification list for watched data assets.

Asset Name	Notification	Details	Modified by	Modified on
Flight Delay	Question Answered	"Yes, it has been standardised! Do let me know if you are looking for anything sp..."	Bobby Simha	Just now
Sales Analysis	Added 3 Stakeholders	Paul Jacobs, Louis Robertson, Ravi Verma	Shalini Chopra	1 hour ago
Airline Sales data	replied to a comment	"this dataset is very useful for my financial ... "	Subashini R	1 hour ago
Hospital Demand anal...	Source Changed	5 Tables deleted in Lineage	Mohan Bonda	1 hour ago
Sales Revenue	Assigned 2 Data Domains	Patient, Address	Prashant	1 hour ago
Customer	Added 3 Stakeholders	Paul Jacobs, Louis Robertson, Ravi Verma	Sudhakshina Vaigundam	1 hour ago
Sales Analysis	Source Changed	5 Tables deleted in Lineage	Peter Haines	2 hours ago
Customer	Assigned 2 Data Domains	Patient, Address	Mila Jokovic	1 day ago

(Notifications — Find)

Figure 5-15. Notifications

The user can elect to have notifications emailed to them as a weekly digest, see Figure 5-16.

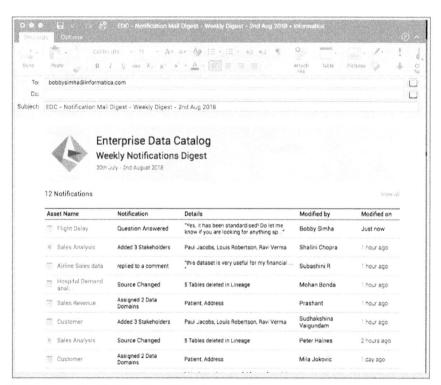

Figure 5-16. Informatica Notifications Digest

Data certification

The data steward can "certify" an asset, publishing the fact to all users that its quality is sufficiently acceptable. This assures users and potential users that this data can be trusted.

The catalog can make data set recommendations to the user based on prior searches and can limit them to certified assets. See Figure 5-17 for Collibra, showing certified assets denoted by a green award ribbon.

Figure 5-17. Recommended certified assets

Some data catalog tools provide a "deprecation" feature similar to certification, which informs users that this data set will be archived or going away. This can also be used to indicate that a scheduled load did not occur and provides a cautionary note to the users of potential problems. See Figure 5-18.

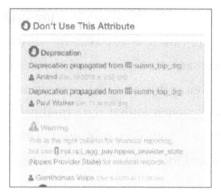

Figure 5-18. Data asset deprecation

Data governance access

Some organizations base data access on the group that a user belongs to; for example, a team of analysts may be assigned to the Sales and Marketing division, so they would be granted access automatically to all the data appropriate for sales and marketing analytics. Permissions are assigned to groups or roles. However, analysts change groups or may be assigned to work on projects other than their normal workload. Then they would need to request access to the new data they need. New data sets have to be analyzed to determine what groups will require it. Often, accesses are not revoked when users transfer, and analysts then still have access to a lot of data that they no longer need, which may be a violation of a data usage agreement.

Users should be able to request access to the data they need. However, how do they find this data if they don't have access to it?

The data catalog can provide an agile approach to data requests. A data catalog can provide access to all assets via metadata, and then a user can request access to data sets which most suit their needs. Customized approval workflows can be put in place for data that have special restrictions. Approvals can be granted for a limited amount of time, and if a user needs it for longer, they can request an extension. Then, when the time has expired, the usage is revoked. Usage can also be restricted if necessary, to a portion of the data that is relevant for the study. This is a much better approach and timesaver for all involved. One of the biggest benefits of this approach is that data quality and governance activities can focus on those data sets being actively used. The catalog can show which assets are used the most and therefore should be managed more closely.

Approval workflow

Workflows are an important process for data governance functions. The level of approvals required may vary, based on the sensitivity of the data and the specific data usage agreements governing a specific data asset. Figure 5-19 contains an example of a data asset approval workflow from Collibra. Collibra supplies over 15 workflows out-of-the-box, with the ability to customize them to fit your own specifications. Figure 5-19 shows several swim lanes representing the parties involved with the approval.

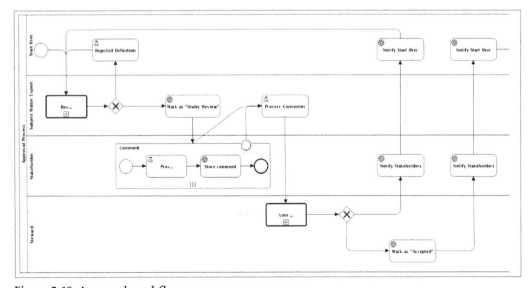

Figure 5-19. Approval workflow

The following scenario demonstrates a simple request and approval process in Collibra.

Shopping for data

Analysts can request access to data through the Collibra Shopping Basket feature. They can add data assets to their shopping basket as shown in Figure 5-20, and when done, click on the Checkout Data Basket button. A summary of each asset is presented. Notice that this particular asset is Certified, shown with the green seal of approval. More about this later in the chapter.

Figure 5-20. Data shopping basket

The user is then presented with a request form that can be used to document usage and business purpose for the understanding of the data owner or steward that will grant access to the assets. See Figure 5-21.

The data steward can then look at the justification and business purpose of the request, and they can approve or reject the request. An example of the request presented to the steward is shown in Figure 5-22. The approval does not automatically give access to the data, instead it triggers the appropriate governance workflow. Actual access must be done via the specific security processes for that data. The data steward can also make notes on the usage and constraints that the user should adhere to.

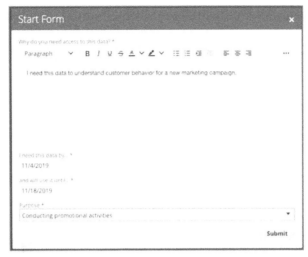

Figure 5-21. Data request form

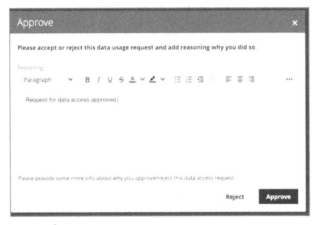

Figure 5-22. Access approval

The analyst is then notified that their request is accepted or rejected. An example of this notification is shown in Figure 5-23. These requests and acceptance communications are governed by a data-sharing agreement between the data owner and the analyst, the details of which are displayed in the notices. The steward acts as a facilitator of communications between the two. The user must accept the notices in order to gain access to the data. The user receives access to the data set via a set of credentials, shown in Figure 5-24.

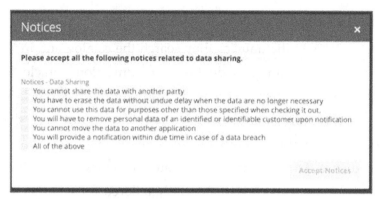

Figure 5-23. Data sharing notices

Figure 5-24. Data usage acceptance credentials

Requesting a change

Users can spot errors in the data, as they search the catalog and in their normal daily use. The catalog can provide the communication vehicle for them to request a business rule change to the appropriate data steward. This can be immensely helpful for data stewards, providing "feet on the ground" intelligence from the users' everyday experiences with the data, acting as additional vigilance. The catalog can then launch a workflow to obtain multiple approvals and consensus if needed, specially tailored for the data set involved. Figure 5-25 provides a pictorial example of how such a request and approval process might work.

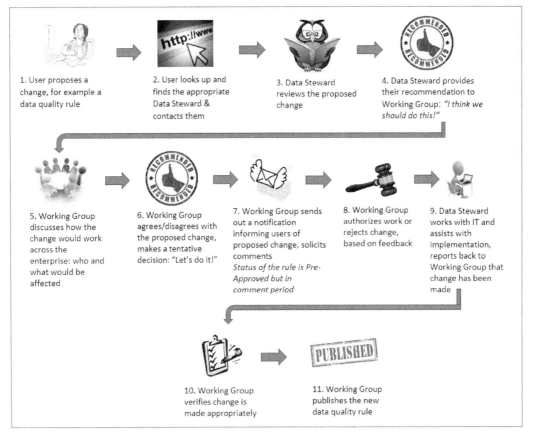

Figure 5-25. Business rule suggestion and approval

The data catalog is the conduit that can facilitate this process, enabling communication between users, data stewards, and working group members, utilizing workflows built into the data governance function in the tool, such as the one shown in Figure 5-19. There would be no need to meet in person because all of the discussion can happen online—in the catalog. The catalog also handles notifications to all the users using the data set, for which the catalog has knowledge. Remember from Chapter 3, we introduced the data catalog chat feature. Figure 5-26 is repeated here from that chapter because it showcases an example of a Conversation from Alation. The user is communicating directly with a data steward to make a data management suggestion concerning an endorsement.

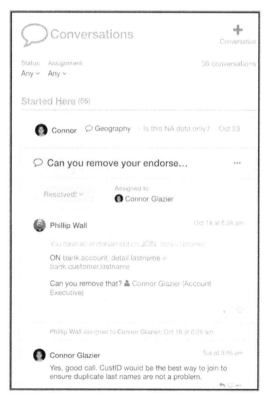

Figure 5-26. Conversation with a data steward

Policies

Data catalogs provide the ability to create and track policies and their enforcement through rules. The European Union's (EU) General Data Protection Regulation (GDPR) is a common policy, specifying that the origin and business purpose of data must be tracked, see Figure 5-27 from Collibra.

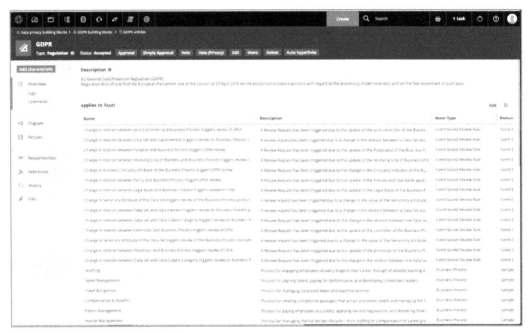

Figure 5-27. Policy example

The policy can have many assets tied to it, including tags, rules, business terms, business domains, and the technical data sets affected by the policy and associated rules. We will discuss this more in Chapter 9 on Data Lineage.

Privacy and risk

An important data governance activity is managing risk. Collibra Privacy & Risk, like Collibra Catalog, is built with governance at the core and on top of the Collibra platform, enabling organizations to implement enterprise data intelligence.

Figure 5-28 presents the integrated Collibra platform and its capabilities.

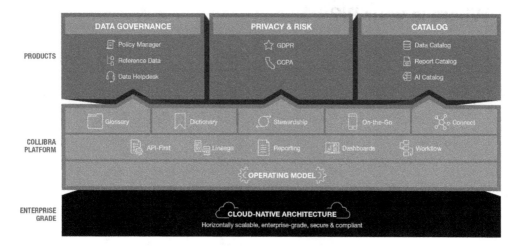

Figure 5-28. Collibra platform

Privacy involves protecting sensitive data. There are strict rules surrounding certain data, such as Personally Identifiable Information (PII). Most tools come with PII as a pre-defined category and some tools have it automatically masked, although you can change this setting.

One of the tasks involved with protecting sensitive information is determining where it exists so that it can be properly managed and tracked. Collibra utilizes ML to discover PII across the organization and map the regulatory and internal policies to the data. This is critical for compliance with major regulations such as GDPR and California Consumer Privacy Act (CCPA). Figure 5-29 shows a lineage diagram in Collibra tracking sensitive data from the policy to the entities in conceptual data models to the physical data locations.

Figure 5-30 shows the identification of a data set as PII in Waterline. Over 300 pre-trained tags can identify sensitive fields, and user-defined rules can be used to employ special controls governing those fields.

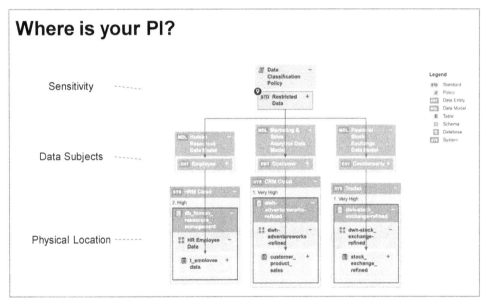

Figure 5-29. Tracing sensitive data

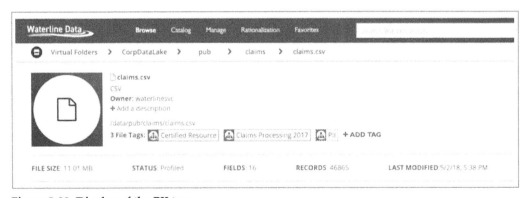

Figure 5-30. Display of the PII tag

Figure 5-31 from Unifi shows Claim Number data masked, so sample data does not show.

Unifi has various protection options, as shown in Figure 5-32. You can set a column as PII, and there are several display options for masking. Permissions can be set for Roles.

yr	123	claim_num...	123	record_id	obc	date_author...	📅	time_author...
2016		**********		D		2016-06-15		08:32:48
2016		**********		D		2016-06-15		13:40:44
2016		**********		D		2016-06-15		16:53:10
2016		**********		D		2016-06-15		17:52:38
2016		**********		D		2016-06-15		15:07:57
2016		**********		D		2016-06-15		15:39:13
2016		**********		D		2016-06-15		07:08:34
2016		**********		D		2016-06-15		11:44:21
2016		**********		D		2016-06-15		19:35:37
2016		**********		D		2016-06-15		14:35:58

Figure 5-31. Claim number as masked

Figure 5-32. Masking display options

You can use as a query the sentence "Show me all the PII" in Unifi, and it will return all data assets containing PII. ML can automatically detect and tag PII based on rules. Certain fields are usually detected as PII, and rules like these come out of the box in most tools, such as a tag for Social Security Number. Unifi has a list of data types that are automatically discovered as PII:

- Credit Card Number
- International Mobile Equipment Identity Number
- IP address (IPV4 and IPV6)
- Email
- Genetic Sequence
- Social Security Number (SSN) (USA)
- Phone Numbers (USA)
- Address (USA)

Informatica offers an add-on product called Secure @ Source, which helps to identify the proliferation of sensitive and PII data. Red dots show that PII data is moving from one place to another and is not protected or masked, and green dots appear in the diagram when data is being controlled, see Figure 5-33.

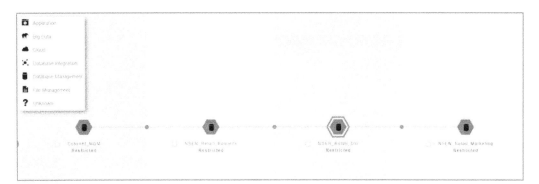

Figure 5-33. PII data controlled

Tags used to label sensitive data can be organized into categories and sub-categories, as shown in Figure 5-34 from Waterline. The high-level category in the glossary is GDPR. This category contains a sub-category tag called Social

Media Data containing tags for Email_address, Linkedin_following, and LinkedIn_Skills.

Figure 5-34. Tag organization in the glossary

Rules can be attached to tags, see Figure 5-35 from Waterline.

The user can create sophisticated rules, see Figure 5-36, also from Waterline. Collibra Privacy & Risk includes a business process register that can be used for any regulation. It also comes with a Discovery and Onboarding capability that allows you to customize your business process register to govern data, applications, systems, and processes. The register ties business and legal context to data. Many regulations mandate that organizations track the business purpose that data was created and used. Individuals under these laws have the right to "be forgotten," which means the organization must be able to delete all data belonging to that individual. This lineage can be performed and the data found using this facility.

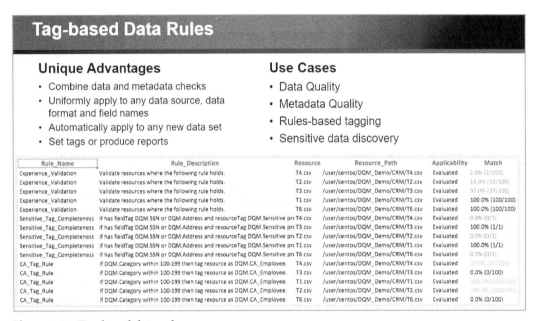

Figure 5-35. Tag-based data rules

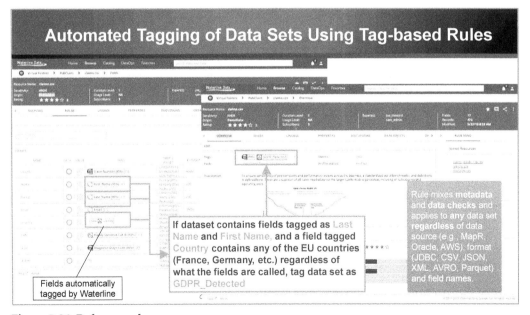

Figure 5-36. Rule example

Collibra's Business Process Discovery and Onboarding can be used when the catalog is first established to find all relevant data to tie to the appropriate business processes and regulations, and it will create the data mappings. It can help you perform risk assessments and remediation planning. It can also be used before a new business process is in place to plan for appropriate privacy measures.

Figure 5-37 shows a Process Asset page from a Register, which shows assets tied to a specific business process that fall under the regulation, in this case, CCPA, shown on the left side of the screen.

Figure 5-37. Process asset page

Collibra provides the ability to set workflows for multiple roles to review and approve data. This may be necessary for extremely sensitive data with specialized Data Usage Agreements (DUAs). Figure 5-38 shows an example of this concept. Different roles will enable multiple processes on Privacy data over time, however, all have access and visibility into the processes.

Figure 5-38. Multiple role review

Key points

This chapter has covered the importance of data governance to the working of the data catalog and effective curation. Data governance should not only be a formal process, but should take advantage of crowdsourcing: The "feet on the ground" intelligence that is provided by the users. These users who interact day to day with the data can provide valuable feedback to the data stewards and become active partners in data governance. Data catalogs offer many strong data governance capabilities, like approval workflows and PII/sensitive data tracking, masking, and management. Many data catalogs have a robust, fully functioning data governance platform along with data quality reporting and dashboards. The data catalog is the perfect vehicle from which to launch data governance because it is directly associated with the data inventory. The ML curation features can partner with the human data steward to enable the best "Goldilocks Data Governance" for the enterprise.

## CHAPTER 6

Fishing in the Data Lake

There is a great influx of streaming data from sensors and the Internet of Things (IoT), retail shopping carts, and other sources. Machine-generated data is partially responsible for this data glut, as machines can generate data much faster than humans, but this is not the only source of large quantities of data. The plethora of data and data types are often termed "Big Data" and are characterized by the 3 V's:

- Velocity: the speed of data flow and processing
- Volume: the amount of data
- Variety: the types and formats of data

These properties began to be circulated back in 2001, describing the complexity of Big Data. The Oxford Lexico Dictionary defines Big Data as:

Extremely large data sets that may be analyzed computationally to reveal patterns, trends, and associations, especially related to human behavior and interactions.[19]

About the data lake

A *data warehouse* is a central repository of data usually sourced from different systems integrated and modeled to enable reporting. *Business Intelligence (BI)*

---

[19] https://www.lexico.com/en/definition/big_data.

refers to reporting and analysis intended to improve business decision-making. One type of BI enables the drill-down of business facts grouped by dimensions; for example, Sales (the facts) by quarter, geographic region, and product type (the dimensions). One specialized data structure used to enable BI reporting is called a *data mart*. New data must be modeled, synchronized, mapped to existing elements, tested for quality, transformed if necessary, and conformed or converted to standard formats such as meters to feet. Reference data must be standardized and mapped accordingly. Data modelers, ETL (Extract, Transform, and Load[20]) developers and database administrators are required to perform specialty work to bring data into the warehouse.

Business analysts working on a tight schedule grew impatient and demanded a faster way to bring data into the environment for analysis, as well as the freedom to explore nuanced relationships between entities outside of the restrictions of a predefined data model. Data marts provided some level of self-service. For example, the analyst could choose which dimensions to drill down. However, the more pressing need was to handle the influx of new data and large volumes in which to run statistical models. Companies started to employ data scientists to create innovative BI reports, data products, and generate insights from enterprise data. These data scientists wanted to run their AI and ML models against a degree of raw data. This coupled with the Big Data characteristics mentioned above, drove the need for large repositories of self-service data.

A *data lake* is a repository of raw data. James Dixon, the founder of Pentaho, coined the term. Here's how he described it in his blog, back in 2010:

---

[20] ETL refers to a class of tools that perform data extract, transforming and loading data from one system into another. These tools are usually graphical in nature and allow mappings to be done with lineage diagrams instead of code.

> *If you think of a datamart as a store of bottled water—cleansed and packaged and structured for easy consumption—the data lake is a large body of water in a more natural state. The contents of the data lake stream in from a source to fill the lake, and various users of the lake can come to examine, dive in, or take samples.*[21]

A data lake is roughly equivalent to an extremely large staging area for a data warehouse and data mart ecosystem, and it is often maintained for such a purpose. However, it is often used as a raw repository for large data sets, the purpose for which has yet to be defined. Large portions of data lakes are commonly used by data scientists to gain insights from data and for investigative purposes.

Data scientists like data lakes because they are unstructured. It is their nature of not requiring data modeling in advance that makes them appealing. However, they can fast become a "dumping ground" where nothing is known about the data therein. It can be said that a data lake that is not well understood and/or governed can quickly become a "data swamp." Therefore, since data is ingested with no modeling or defined schema upfront, a data lake is not usually well understood because it lacks descriptive metadata. The data is stored there so it can be studied. The aspiration is that studying it will bring understanding.

Data lake data catalog

A data catalog can be immensely helpful in enabling governance of data and making sense of data lakes and Big Data. It can be reasonably argued that a data

---

[21] Quoted in Gorelik, Alex. The Enterprise Big Data Lake. 2019: O'Reilly Media Inc., page 2. Original Source: https://jamesdixon.wordpress.com/2010/10/14/pentaho-hadoop-and-data-lakes/.

catalog is intrinsic to data lake success. Gartner predicts in its research that data lake projects will fail without a method of inventorying data:

> *"Through 2022, over 80% data lake projects will fail to deliver value as finding, inventorying and curating data will prove to be the biggest inhibitor to analytics and data science success."*[22]

We believe industry analysts are united on the imperative to employing data management discipline and governance in the deployment of data lakes. Data lakes often atrophy when there is no data management governing the data within it.

Consider the following scenarios:

- A data lake is created for a specific project. Data is ingested, and the number of analysts dealing with it are limited and work closely together. They collaborate naturally and figure out issues with the data together. The data for the project remains in the lake after the project is completed, although it is not used or cataloged. Several months later, analysts work on a similar project and could have found the original data useful, but they didn't know of its existence. They end up locating similar data from another source and duplicating much of the efforts of the previous analysts in figuring out the data.

- A new executive joins the organization and believes the future is in data lakes. They establish an enterprise data lake—all new analytic projects feed their data into the lake. However, there is no way to quickly determine what data resides there. Analysts end up performing manual

---

[22] Gartner. "Augmented Data Catalogs: Now an Enterprise Must-Have for Data and Analytics Leaders," Ehtisham Zaidi, September 12, 2019. ID: G00394570.

queries on the various folders containing data. There's no indication of where the data came from or what its original purpose was. Analysts are spending considerable time trying to decipher what data is in the lake and whether it is fit for their purpose. This story is similar to the story in Chapter 2 where the data analyst did not know where to go to get the data for her study.

The moral of these stories is just because you have a data lake, does not mean you have useful data.

Data warehouses are often accompanied by solid data management, including:

- Data governance
- Data descriptions such as data dictionaries
- Data modeling
- Semantic data mapping and data integration
- Master and reference data management
- Data quality
- Life cycle management including an archive strategy
- Metadata management

A data lake is an essential infrastructure and hosting platform. It is not a data management strategy and does not inherently build in data governance.

How, then, can some data management rigor be applied to a data lake and at the same time, realize the major benefits of fast, large-volume data ingest and no limiting, prescribed storage schema?

The answer is through the judicious use of a data catalog coupled with both machine and human curation.

A data catalog that can help bring order and understanding to a data lake needs to be able to handle large volumes and still help make sense of ambiguity. Such a tool needs to effectively use ML to curate more and more data with a high degree of accuracy as well as enable human input towards deciphering ingested data.

An example of a product that specializes in this area is Waterline Data.

Example: Waterline Data from Hitachi Vantara

Manual attempts to create data inventories can fail under normal circumstances, but in the world of Big Data, it is impossible to keep up with the voluminous influx, variety, and velocity of new data. Big Data requires automation and scalability. Figure 6-1 from Waterline Data illustrates how this product fulfills these requirements. Note that the data catalog brings together business and technical metadata, with ML driving the process. The catalog collects technical metadata when data is ingested (and when data is changed) using automation, and users supply business metadata and context including terms and governance/compliance policies and rules.

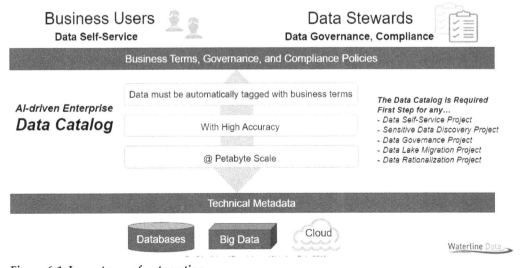

Figure 6-1. Importance of automation

The data catalog must have a high degree of automation and ML and still be able to scale. Although this is discussed in Chapter 7 in the context of the enterprise data catalog, it is even more critical when dealing with data lakes and Big Data. Automation is essential, but it must also be partnered with human curation. The information in the catalogs must be curated both by data stewards and "feet on the ground" analysts, the business users, who are working with the data day-to-day. The ML recommendations may be incorrect, so they must be confirmed and approved by a human.

There must be a partnership. Based on the knowledge in the catalog, the ML recommends tags for assets as they are ingested. Then, as the data is being used, crowdsourcing enables business users, analysts, and data stewards to approve the ML recommendations. Users must also be able to create new tags and/or make additional assignments of existing tags. These new tags and assignments are added to the overall body of knowledge in the catalog, and the ML algorithms get "smarter" from this new knowledge and can make even more recommendations with greater accuracy. See Figure 6-2.

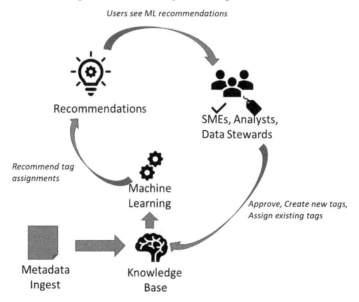

Figure 6-2. Partnership between human and ML

Fishing features

Glossary

A glossary is a list of terms approved by data stewards to be the language of the business. Most data catalog products provide a way of importing a glossary and enabling a hierarchy of terms, usually subdivided by subject areas or business domains, such as Finance or Sales/Marketing.

Most products also enable collaborative curation of the glossary and have approved terms versus proposed terms or candidates. Chapter 7 will cover this subject in more depth. ML augmented catalogs can automatically tag fields with business terms from the glossary so they can be used in searches to return the related technical metadata, see Figure 6-3.

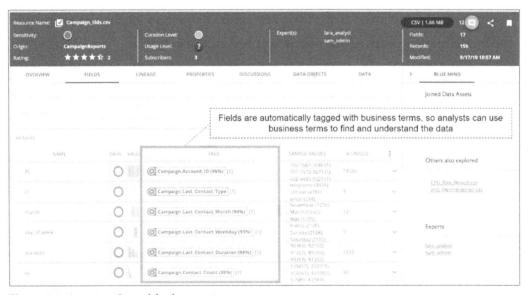

Figure 6-3. Auto tagging with glossary terms

"Fingerprinting"

The name of Waterline's ML engine is Aristotle. Aristotle creates a "fingerprint" for every data asset ingested. Figure 6-4 illustrates Aristotle's fingerprinting and how it is used.

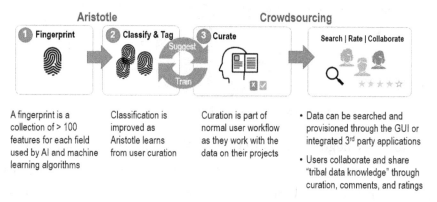

A fingerprint is a collection of > 100 features for each field used by AI and machine learning algorithms

Classification is improved as Aristotle learns from user curation

Curation is part of normal user workflow as they work with the data on their projects

- Data can be searched and provisioned through the GUI or integrated 3rd party applications
- Users collaborate and share "tribal data knowledge" through curation, comments, and ratings

Like a human analyst, the more Aristotle learns, the better it becomes

Figure 6-4. Fingerprinting at work

Subject Matter Experts (SMEs) and data stewards can add business terms to the glossary, which can be curated like other data assets—business terms can be suggested by users and approved by data stewards. The glossary grows as new terms are added, organization of the data assets becomes more well-defined, and terms gain deeper meaning and can be better understood.

Figure 6-3 and Figure 6-4 illustrated the partnership between human and machine. Another way to visualize this is shown in Figure 6-5. Aristotle's ML fingerprints the data. Users associate existing business terms with data and create new terms, adding to the glossary. Aristotle matches fingerprints of already tagged fields with the fingerprints of other data, suggesting that the tag also applies to the data belonging to the fingerprint, and provides a confidence factor. Users see that the tag is a suggestion and can accept or reject the match. The results of the human curation are fed into ML, training the algorithm with the new knowledge.

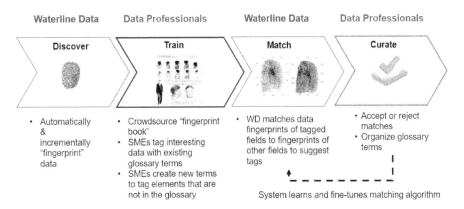

Figure 6-5. Using fingerprints to expand the knowledge base

Tags are informal categories and are used in Waterline, like most data catalogs, to create a folksonomy that users can employ to find data assets. Tags can be associated with rules. Maintenance of tags can be a challenge. What happens to tags when new rules or new tags are added? Can you delete tags? Many data catalog products require a new scan of the data when new rules are added, which is resource-intensive and can negatively impact performance. Figure 6-6 shows how Waterline handles tags through its fingerprinting process.

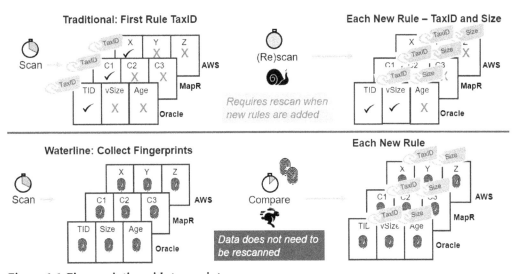

Figure 6-6. Fingerprinting aids tag maintenance

Each fingerprint is treated as a unique element. Fingerprints are compared, and there is no need for a rescan.

Data profiling

Waterline makes extensive use of data profiling to help business users and data analysts understand what the data contains, and it uses profiling to add metadata to the fingerprints. *Data Profiling*, sometimes called descriptive analytics, is the:

- systematic,
- methodical,
- repeatable,
- non-specific,
- non-directed,
- metrics-based, and
- usually automated evaluation of data.

Data profiling provides technical metadata that is descriptive enough to offer clues to further decipher the context of the data, thereby aiding in the discovery of business metadata.

Data profiling can provide the following information about columns in a database table:

- Data type (both defined and inferred)

- The minimum value (as sorted by alphanumeric character set)

- The maximum value

- The number of unique values (if this equals the number of rows in the table, the field is 100% unique and is a primary key[23] or unique identifier candidate)

- Selectivity, is derived from the number of unique values divided by the total number of rows

- Number of Nulls[24] (unknowns)

- Density, is determined by the percent of Nulls. If a column has no nulls, it has a density of 1 or 100%

- DateTime Count, which counts the number of values in the field with a date and/or date time

- String count

The profiling results also show pattern distributions, which are exceedingly helpful, especially in fields containing strings and freeform text.

Figure 6-7 is an example of Waterline's Fields tab showing details of an obscurely named field, MA90. The profiling results, coupled with the suggested tag and the patterns discovered in the data, paint a picture of what the data in this field means. The tag suggested is Agent ID with an 86% confidence factor.

---

[23] A **Primary key** is used in relational database tables to join one principle table to a secondary, detail table, for example, an Order ID would be the Primary Key in an Order Header table and would appear in a detail table such as Order Details, which would allow the detail rows such as the products purchased to be associated with the date of the order.

[24] **Null** is a value used in a database column to represent the fact that data in the column is "unknown" or not applicable in some way. It is not the same thing as an empty field but may have a similar meaning. Summaries often cannot be performed properly if nulls exist, and the developer usually must convert them to zero or to another value to perform the summary.

The data captured in the field is mixed, with the highest count pattern indicating a numeric value, the second-highest count pattern indicates a string of only alpha characters. Clearly, this field needs to be investigated further. Perhaps Agent IDs are not uniform in type, but can be either all alphas or all numeric?

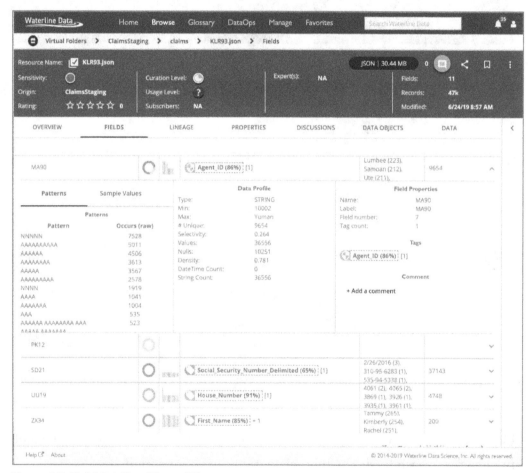

Figure 6-7. Field details with profiling

The screen displays a colored circle indicating the type of data (purple means it is a string). Null values must also be considered. A purple circle whose perimeter is not filled in completely indicates string values but with gray coloring to indicate the percent null in the field. Figure 6-8 shows a close-up of this null distribution indicating the field is about 25% null. This would raise a red flag for a field that is supposed to contain an identifier.

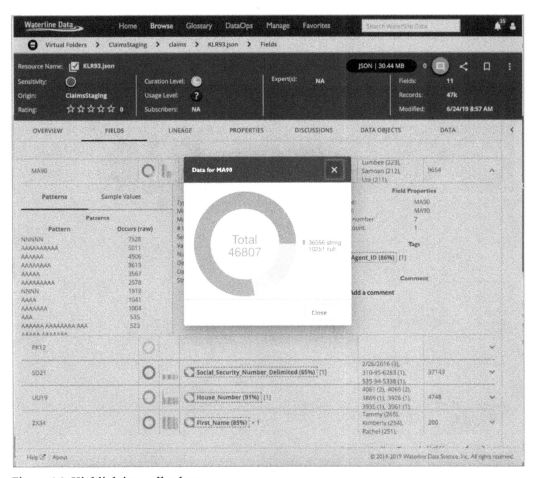

Figure 6-8. Highlighting null values

Figure 6-9 shows mini histograms providing visual representations of value frequencies in each field. The mini histogram can be expanded.

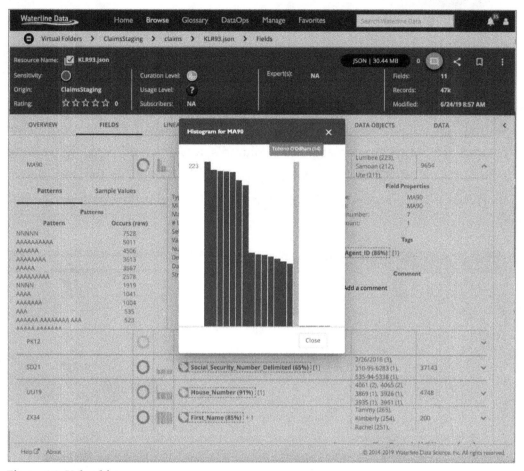

Figure 6-9. Value histogram

Notice that the value that appears the most is found 223 times. The profiling screen in Figure 6-10 shows this value is the character string "Lumbee." The histogram shows there is a group of high appearing values, and then there's a group of lesser appearing values. The number of nulls (shown in the gray bar) exceeds the highest count value.

We can also look at alphabetical order and see the minimum (or first in alpha order) is a numeric value, and the maximum value is a string beginning with "Y," "Yuman." Often, anomalies will show up at either end of the spectrum, such as the entry "99999," which can indicate another way to express Null, or an unknown value.

Figure 6-10 shows another interesting example of data profiling in Waterline. This column detail screen also appeared in the first chapter but is repeated here to highlight an interesting profiling result. The profiling results for a given column are shown underneath that column's row—in this case, the column featured is called "CV56." The column names in this table, like the ones shown in Figure 6-10, provide no information about what the data in the columns represent.

Figure 6-10. Another data profiling example showing emails in a field

Notice that this column, based on the sample data, appears to contain last names, but the pattern frequency distribution tells a different story. There appears to be emails buried in the field. They are infrequent but they do exist, and probably represent overloading. Overloading means use of a field for a purpose other than that which it was originally designed. This probably represents a data quality problem that may have to be dealt with later. It is interesting that Aristotle does not recommend a tag for this field. The fact that no recommendation was made may be very significant and could indicate that the data steward should possibly focus their efforts on columns with no recommendations. It may indicate, as it does in Figure 6-10, that there is a conflict in the data that exists in the field, and human curation may be required. Both recommendations and the lack thereof have significance for understanding data and have data governance ramifications.

Data catalog products vary in how they conduct data profiling and display profiling results. Data profiling should be done upon metadata ingest, and some products can rescan the data periodically in case the data changes. Some catalogs have automated means of detecting data changes and recalculating profile results. Others regenerate a sample when a user brings up the catalog page for that asset, in order to keep the sample fresh, but may have performance issues. Some products only provide profile statistics on a sample. Many catalogs display sample data (if the user has permission to view it). Sample data is helpful, but a profile done on the entire data set is most informative. A sample is usually not a reliable indication of what is really in the entire data set. It provides a quick look and may lead to false assumptions.

A nuance in data profiling involves hierarchical data such as JSON or XML. Traditional data profiling works well with relational tables, but there can be issues when it is applied to hierarchies. Tools use a technique called shredding, which creates a logical field containing each level of the hierarchy. Shredding is imperfect because it is "lossy," it loses information. This happens when there are multiple values in one of the hierarchies, such as two customers and five products on a single order. A traditional shredding method would create ten rows—one row for each combination of customers and products. When this shredded data is profiled, the statistics for the value counts for each product, for example, would be severely skewed. The tools differ in how they handle this.

Waterline profiles hierarchical data natively. In the orders example, it would treat and profile two customers as two separate rows and five products as five different rows, thus preserving accurate statistics.

Data profiling results are used to populate fingerprints, for example, see Figure 6-11. The fingerprint contains the field name and all the profile results for the field, including the minimum value, maximum value, and mean for a numeric field. It also contains the context, the other fields in the table, and associated values.

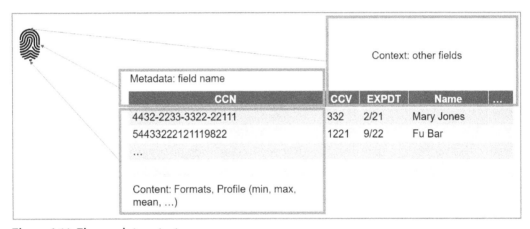

Figure 6-11. Fingerprint contents

Data connections

Many times, a business user or data analyst may want to bring together several data sources that have never been combined before, as was faced by one of the authors of this book several months ago! The question then becomes how to do this and if it is even possible. Does a column or combination of columns exist so that there might be enough overlap between the two sources to join them reliably? Data enrichment possibilities surface, such as performing a study on longevity and geographic areas using a data set with state and national park locations. Do people live longer who live near a park? You might be able to bring together these data sets if you had longitude and latitude information. You must also factor whether the data sets overlap. If you have demographics on people who live in one state, and you have parks in another state, they don't overlap and would not be helpful.

Tools can help identify potential joins in several different ways:

- Relational databases use primary and foreign keys to join database tables, as discussed above. The unique identifier from one table (primary key) is used to join with the foreign key in the other table. Courses taught in a college would have a foreign key called Professor ID, which links to the primary key in the Professor table. The data catalog can easily connect these two tables since this linkage is already defined in the database (called an integrity constraint). More often than not, there is no constraint defined but the tool can still infer the join because of the names.

- Names of joined columns might be the same. In our Courses/Professor example, the Courses table might have a column called Professor ID, and this column would also exist in the Professor table. The data types would also be the same.

- The catalog contains a lot of intelligence about data usage, and there may be joins that already exist in other data assets, such as ETL code, queries, database/federated views, and reports.

- Tags can be used to infer like data. This is a creative way that the catalog can make guesses as to what joins might be possible, especially with data sets that have never been brought together before. This is where fingerprinting can come in.

The identification of potential join conditions across heterogeneous data is a very useful feature, and Figure 6-11 shows how Waterline's fingerprinting does this, see Figure 6-12. Once a join is constructed, it can be materialized as a Hive table if all data sets are in Apache Hadoop, S3, or other environments that support Hive. Waterline is working on supporting Presto for heterogeneous joins—an open-source distributed SQL query engine for Big Data.

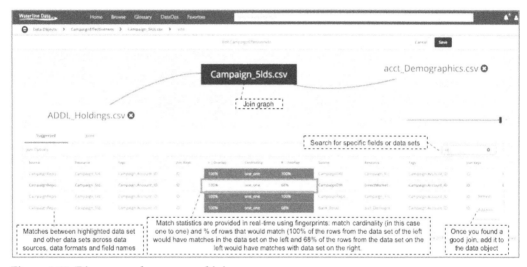

Figure 6-12. Discover and recommend joins

Data origin and lineage

The GDPR regulation from the EU, defined in Chapter 5, requires that the origin and business purpose of data be tracked. See Figure 6-13.

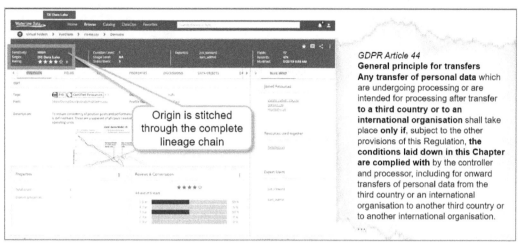

Figure 6-13. Data origin

You can create custom properties in Waterline to capture compliance metadata such as Business Purpose, and the user can search on it, see Figure 6-14.

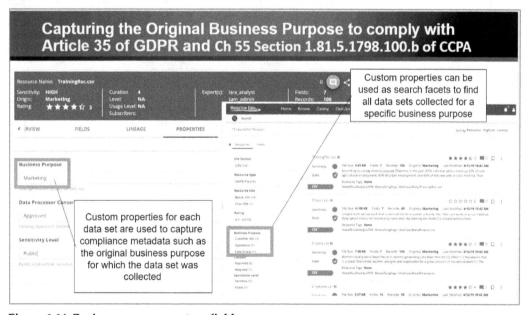

Figure 6-14. Business purpose custom field

Lineage can be imported using REST APIs and connectors. Fingerprints can be used to infer and construct missing lineage, see Figure 6-15.

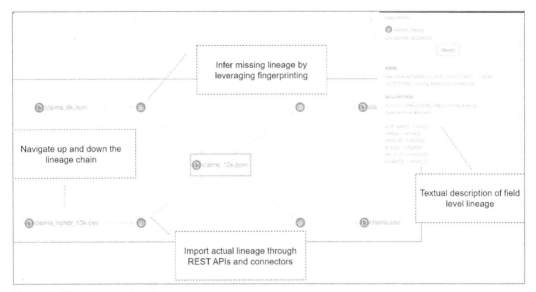

Figure 6-15. Infer missing lineage

Fingerprints can also be used to find duplicates. The data steward can identify a data set as Primary, Copy, or Deprecated. This is very helpful for the analyst and saves them time and frustration by avoiding the use of a deprecated source. See Figure 6-16.

Figure 6-16. Identifying duplicates

Avoid siloed data catalogs

Some forward-looking data scientists have discovered the utilitarian benefits of analysis tools and data catalogs for data lakes. They have consequently deployed siloed data catalogs along with a dedicated data lake for their singular purpose. This resembles the data warehouse craze a decade ago, where a single department would deploy a data warehouse specifically for their needs and not for the whole enterprise. Alex Gorelik, author of *The Enterprise Big Data Lake*, has named these dedicated data lakes "data puddles." Chief Data Officers and Enterprise Data Architects should evaluate the need for an enterprise data catalog that would span data puddles and examine their use cases. An isolated data catalog can help add context and meaning to the data to be sure, but the biggest value in data catalog technology is helping analysts locate and understand "dark data," the data in the enterprise that is not documented and hard to find.

Scaling to an enterprise data catalog is shown in Figure 6-17. Waterline can span across the entire ecosystem using Agents running natively on Spark clusters or in containers using the Kubernetes framework.

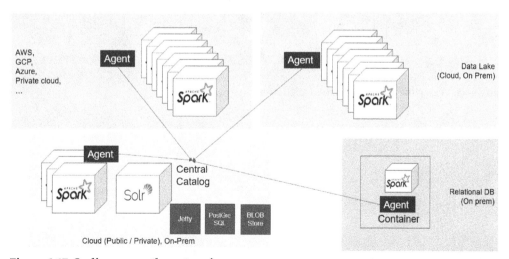

Figure 6-17. Scaling across the enterprise

Key points

The data catalog, as we have seen in this chapter, has immense power to help understand and curate Big Data and data lakes. It can provide a window into the data and, at the same time, help ingest and curate large volumes of complex data. Figure 6-18 summarizes the value of a data catalog especially in the challenging data lake environment. The partnership between human and ML both for search and curation cannot be underestimated, and will be the focus of Chapter 10.

Figure 6-18. Waterline big data search facilitation

CHAPTER 7

One-Stop Shopping

The emphasis in this book is on the importance of a data catalog that is enterprise-wide, enabling searches that span silos. Such a catalog bridges these silos and makes data all over the enterprise discoverable, perhaps for the very first time. Some of the vendors and industry analysts call this the discovery of "dark data"—data that exists, but nobody knows it is there.

An enterprise data catalog, therefore, needs to:

- Support the scanning of large volumes of data
- Ingest a diversity of data types, formats (structured or unstructured) and platforms (on-premises, cloud, or hybrid cloud)
- Make this data understandable to both technical and non-technical users
- Facilitate searches across the diverse data types using ML
- Automate curation with ML

It seems like a natural expansion of functionality that an enterprise data catalog would offer more than just a data inventory but extend its reach to encompass enterprise data management functionality as well. The catalog's curation functionality blends well with data governance, as we saw in Chapter 5. Most of the major data management disciplines involve data governance, such as:

- Data quality, overseeing quality improvements and rules, ensuring that it increases over time

- Reference data and Master Data Management (MDM), putting standards and rules in place for master and reference consistency throughout the enterprise

- Data Integration, ensuring data is properly matched with similar data in other systems in the enterprise when it is brought together for summaries, ensuring that summaries are accurate

It could, therefore, be argued that a true enterprise data catalog is more than just a catalog. It expands and serves all the major data management disciplines in one unified platform.

Both IBM and Informatica initially offered specific data management products and tools, and then expanded their respective offerings by acquisition and in-house development. They both now offer complete data management platforms, which include a data catalog at their center. This chapter presents examples of both to illustrate expansive enterprise data catalog features, focusing on each one in turn then interspersed to spotlight different capabilities. We are calling this class of tools the One-Stop Shop.

Enterprise data catalogs

Most data catalog tools have evolved from other data-centric tools that were designed for a specific use case or solution. Although tools of this nature are often limited by their use case focus area and therefore difficult to add features, IBM and Informatica are exceptions.

An enterprise data catalog must be able to bridge silos and span across many different environments and sources. The "One-Stop Shop" catalog products do this. Both vendors have worked hard to ingest disparate sources that are not native to their respective platforms. Figure 7-1 from Informatica illustrates the various disparate sources and platforms that need to be supported by an enterprise catalog in order to be effective. The due diligence you perform when researching catalog products for purchase must include a checklist for infrastructure and source types within your environment.

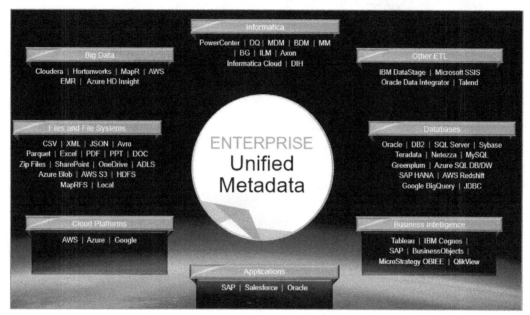

Figure 7-1. Types of sources and platforms in Informatica

There are two considerations for infrastructure: what the catalog runs on and what the ingest sources run on. An enterprise data catalog must be able to access a wide variety of data sources and also scale. See Figure 7-2 from Informatica, illustrating both diversity of ingest platforms and the CLAIRE platform on a high-performance parallel architecture (Hadoop cluster).

A prospective buyer needs to keep this in mind and determine not just the sources that will be ingested but also the infrastructure upon which the catalog resides. Catalog performance is dependent upon its underlying architecture, facilitating its ability to scan to profile data sources and perform ML algorithms in real-time.

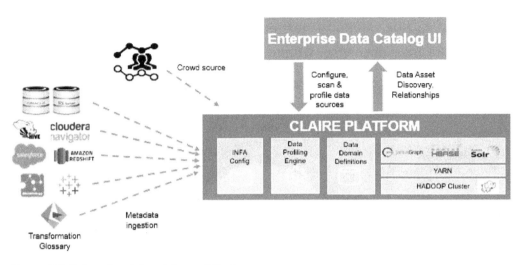

Figure 7-2. Enterprise data catalog architecture

Example: IBM

IBM created one of the first relational databases, DB2, and before that, IBM was known for mainframes and mainframe databases such as Information Management System (IMS). C.J. Date was one of the founders of relational theory, and he hailed from IBM. Then IBM acquired and built an entire suite of database management products under the InfoSphere umbrella, including the acquisition of Ascential bringing DataStage, ProfileStage, QualityStage and others; Master Data Management, including an in-house tool and the acquisition of Initiate; and others, including Information Governance, workflow, and Business Glossary. IBM introduced the Information Governance Catalog (IGC), a data catalog product with its main focus being data governance.

The integration of these capabilities has been challenging for IBM, but they have finally succeeded with many of them shown in Figure 7-3.

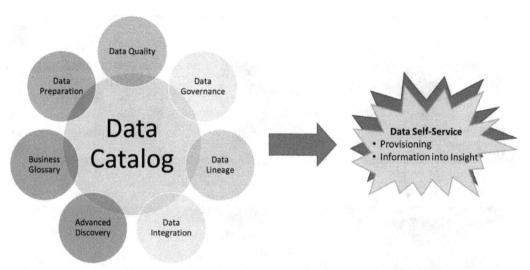

Figure 7-3. Integrated data catalog

IBM added its powerful AI engine Watson to this platform. You'll recall that Watson was the famous AI question-answering computer that won the *Jeopardy* TV game show's grand prize of $1 Million in 2011.[25] The Watson AI engine has been incorporated into many different products and services. IBM offered Watson Knowledge Catalog (WKC), an ML-empowered data catalog that was initially not integrated with the rest of the InfoSphere data management products. Bringing WKC together with IGC and the InfoSphere suite resulted in an enterprise data catalog and one-stop shop for data management. This is a fully integrated data platform called Cloud Pak for Data. Watson's technology is employed not just in the data catalog but also Watson's data prep (Watson Applications), Watson Studio, Watson Machine Learning, and Watson OpenScale. The Cloud Pak for Data platform encompasses all the data management capabilities embedded in the InfoSphere product line coupled with the Watson products, enabling data self-service to drastically reduce time to insight. See Figure 7-4.

---

[25] https://tek.io/2GzWiJk.

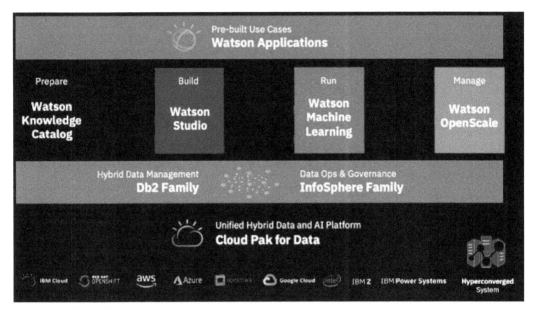

Figure 7-4. IBM Cloud Pak for Data

Figure 7-5 shows a deeper dive into IBM's many capabilities and components, showing five core operations driving a business-ready data pipeline:

- Metadata curation services: Watson Knowledge Catalog

- Metadata Management: Infosphere augmented with Watson ML

- Self-services interaction: catalog functions enabling collaboration and data citizen curation: Watson Knowledge Catalog

- Core governance and master data management: Information Governance Catalog plus IBM Master Data Management

- Machine learning and automation: Watson ML

The InfoSphere suite brings the data management functions of data quality, MDM, data integration, and data governance, together with Watson and IGC all into one platform. This complete platform delivers the Business Ready Supply Chain. See Figure 7-6.

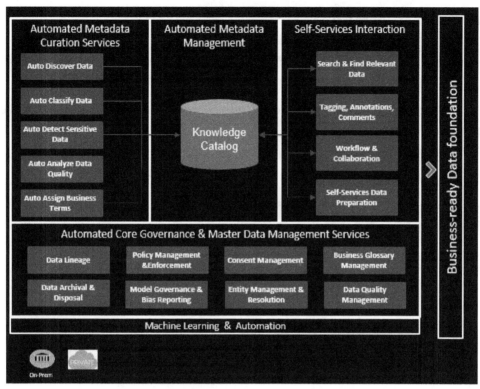

Figure 7-5. IBM capabilities and components

Enterprise Data Integration	Enterprise Data Quality	Enterprise Data Governance	Enterprise Data Consumption
IBM provides the most comprehensive, most integrated, and most scalable data integration platform provides the core data integration backbone running in the largest banks, telcos, retailers, insurance companies, etc.	IBM provides the most complete, most scalable, and most integrated data quality platform supporting data profiling; creation, execution, and monitoring of data validation rules and data matching and consolidation.	IBM provides an enterprise data governance platform that supports business and technical users on data governance teams. It eliminates the cost and complexity of integrating a stand-alone data governance platforms with data integration, quality, and consumption tooling.	IBM provides an enterprise data catalog that delivers self-service capabilities for data citizens (business analysts, data scientists) to search and explore information, to preview and refine information to act upon information in a secure environment driving new data science or analytics.

Figure 7-6. IBM's Business Ready Supply Chain

Example: Informatica

Informatica has been on a very similar adventure. Known in the early days of data warehousing for its extremely powerful ETL suite of tools (PowerCenter), Informatica was the first vendor to introduce an ETL product that had a server, scheduler, workflow, and lineage support. It was a natural extension for Informatica to produce graphical lineage from their ETL jobs and packages, and they released various iterations of a metadata tool. Today, like IBM, they offer a comprehensive data management platform but as a smorgasbord of coordinated plug-and-play components, bringing a powerful integrated solution. See Figure 7-7.

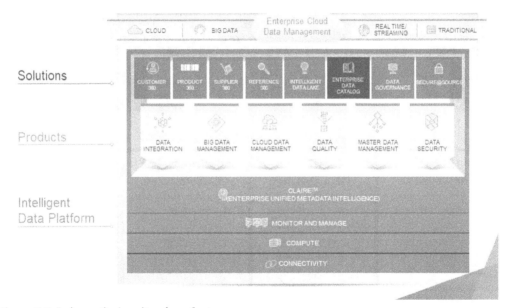

Figure 7-7. Informatica's suite of products

Informatica has CLAIRE, mentioned above, with AI in the middle of its name: The AI engine empowering ML to assist both curation and search.

Informatica's integrated suite of products includes:

- Business Glossary
- Data Quality
- Data Profiling
- Data Integration
- Big Data support
- Master/Reference Data Management
- Data governance, including workflow
- Security

Figure 7-8 shows a more detailed look into how the various components are integrated into the platform to deliver a complete data management solution.

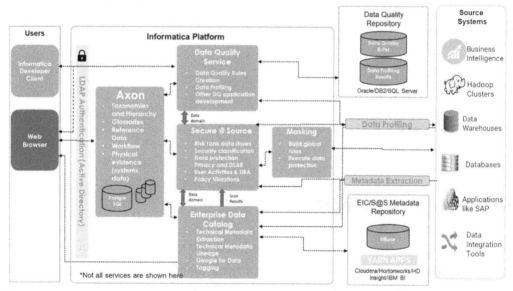

Figure 7-8. Informatica components: deep dive

The way Informatica offers their products differs from IBM. IBM sells them as a bundle, Cloud Pak for Data, and Informatica offers them as separate components. The latter's philosophy is that customers should be able to choose the components they want.

It is obvious that both products would offer strong integration with their own tools. Data lineage and visibility into transformations within the Informatica PowerCenter has always been strong. See Figure 7-9, which shows a portion of a data flow. The expression used in the output field is displayed by selecting the icon shown in Figure 7-9. See Chapter 9 for a detailed discussion of data lineage. Data integration is best displayed as lineage diagrams.

Figure 7-9. Lineage depicted as a data flow

Reference data support

Reference data is used to organize or categorize other data. Often, reference data includes code sets that serve as shorthand for longer named elements. They are extremely helpful, especially for relational databases, because they avoid redundancy and typographical errors. A reference data table contains the codes, their values, and descriptions. An application that requires the data specified in the code set would only use the code, and a join in the database would bring the description to the requesting application. The beauty of this system is that codes are maintained in one central place.

Figure 7-10 from Informatica shows the types of reference data that can exist in an organization.

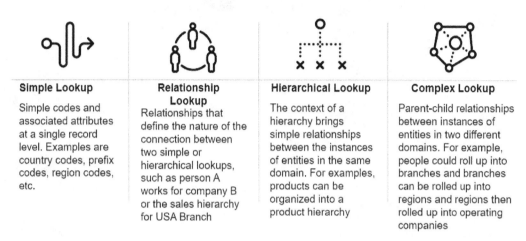

Simple Lookup	Relationship Lookup	Hierarchical Lookup	Complex Lookup
Simple codes and associated attributes at a single record level. Examples are country codes, prefix codes, region codes, etc.	Relationships that define the nature of the connection between two simple or hierarchical lookups, such as person A works for company B or the sales hierarchy for USA Branch	The context of a hierarchy brings simple relationships between the instances of entities in the same domain. For examples, products can be organized into a product hierarchy	Parent-child relationships between instances of entities in two different domains. For example, people could roll up into branches and branches can be rolled up into regions and regions then rolled up into operating companies

Figure 7-10. Types of reference data

Issues occur, however, when different applications use different sets of codes for the same data. For example, suppose an enterprise tracks projects, and each department has a different set of codes that represent the status of a project. Here's the Sales Department's code set:

Table 7-1. Sales Department Project Codes

Code	Value	Description
100	Proposed	The project has been scoped and proposed to management.
200	Pending	The project has been submitted and is waiting for approval.
300	Approved	The project has been approved.
400	Active	The project is underway.
500	Canceled	The project has been canceled.
600	Completed	The project has been completed.

Here's the IT Department's code set:

Table 7-2. IT Department Project Codes

Code	Value	Description
I	Initiated	The project is in the proposal phase.
U	Under Review	The proposal is under review.
S	Submitted for Approval	The project has been submitted for approval.
P	Pending	The project is on hold.
A	Approved	The project has been approved.
D	Denied	The project has been rejected and approval is not granted.
O	Active	The project is active and ongoing.
X	Canceled	The project has been canceled.
C	Completed	The project has been completed.

Notice that these code lists are different from each other and may not map easily. The organization would need to determine how they want to report on projects enterprise-wide.

Figure 7-11 shows a graphic from Informatica illustrating the mapping problem from three different systems, and three different code sets. The tool will maintain these mappings to the enterprise codes. Fortunately, standards bodies exist to create standardized lists of codes that many organizations use. For example, the International Standards Organization (ISO) maintains several lists of geographic codes such as countries in the world. They maintain 3166 Country Codes[26] and several varieties based on length and whether subdivisions (such as US States) are included. However, even when using these lists, you must ensure you specify the issuing standards organization.

---

[26] https://www.iso.org/iso-3166-country-codes.html.

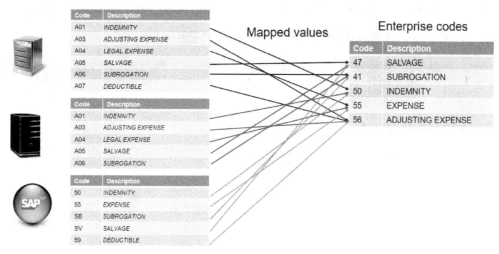

Figure 7-11. Reference data mapping

It can be an interesting problem when different standards bodies maintain the same type of reference data. At least three standards bodies maintain "standard" lists of airport codes:

- International Air Transport Association (IATA)
- International Civil Aviation Organization (ICAO)
- Federal Aviation Administration (FAA)

The FAA maintains only airport codes for airports in the United States, so it contains no international codes. Sometimes the three code sets will agree, and sometimes they differ. Harmonization of reference data is important for enterprise data management. Data catalog tools help maintain and provide visibility into reference data mappings.

One-Stop Shop tools provide a window into reference data management and governance. Reference data in IBM WKC can be either imported from a Comma Separated Values (CSV) file or entered manually. WKC provides a simple drag and drop interface, very familiar to Excel users, see Figure 7-12. You drag and drop the fields into the three categories of metadata: Code, Value and Description, just as you would in an Excel file import.

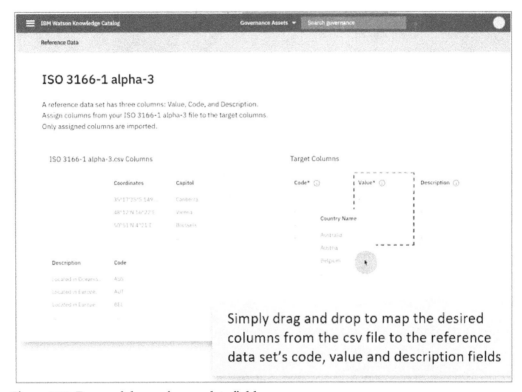

Figure 7-12. Drag and drop reference data fields

You can then see the results of the import in Figure 7-13.

Reference data can get very complicated. Some reference data is in a hierarchical form, such as the medical diagnostic code set International Statistical Classification of Diseases (ICD-10). Other examples are product hierarchies and organizational charts. Informatica provides support for hierarchical code sets with versioning and collaboration, see Figure 7-14.

Code ⌃	Value	Description
AUS	Australia	Located in Oceania.
AUT	Austria	Located in Europe
BEL	Belgium	Located in Europe
CAN	Canada	Located in North America
CHN	China	Located in Asia
DNK	Denmark	Located in Europe
FIN	Finland	Located in Europe
FRA	France	Located in Europe
GHA	Ghana	Located in Africa
MAR	Morocco	Located in Africa

Items per page: **10** ▾ | 1 - 10 of 40 items

Figure 7-13. Reference data imported

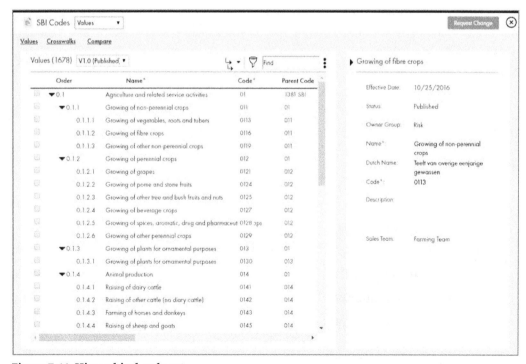

Figure 7-14. Hierarchical code set

Business glossary

IBM has a well-developed Business Glossary component, with both searching and editing term capabilities. The workflow follows the author's Governance Lite™27 methodology which is a lightweight governance framework specially designed for glossary terms. It is reactive governance, allowing users to enter terms or modify descriptions that are then sent to the data steward for approval. A search for terms will show the status of the term, see Figure 7-15. This search revealed a term called Alternate Service Identifier, which shows a status of Inactive, highlighted in pink.

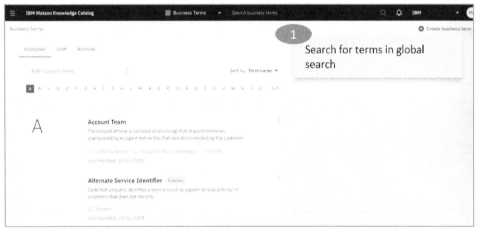

Figure 7-15. Glossary search

The user can edit the description or create a new term (see the "Create business term" at the top right corner) in Figure 7-15. The status of the term changes to "Draft" shown in blue right after the term name when an edit is made, see Figure 7-16. The user can then submit it for approval (upper right box) or delete their changes. The submittal activates the term governance workflow by notifying the appropriate data steward.

---

27 Governance Lite™ was introduced in this online newsletter: https://bit.ly/2Gu7bMy.

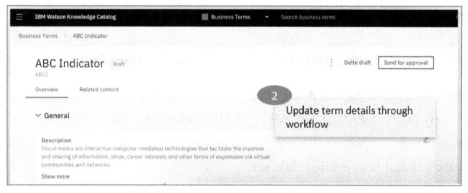

Figure 7-16. Update a term

Term relationships

Figure 7-17 shows the user's ability to specify relationships between terms, including the ability to have type hierarchies. This is very powerful and can greatly assist searches by retrieving related assets. It not only shows that a term is related but also how they are related. Elaborate hierarchies can be established.

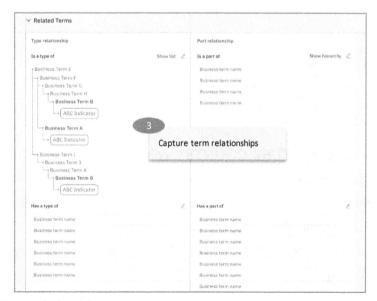

Figure 7-17. Term relationships

Data quality support

Both vendors offer integration with their data quality products.

Figure 7-18 shows the start of a data quality investigation in Informatica. The user surveys the CRM_CUSTOMER_MAIN table associated with the business term "Customer." Notice the green "seal of approval" next to the table name, indicating that it is a certified data set.

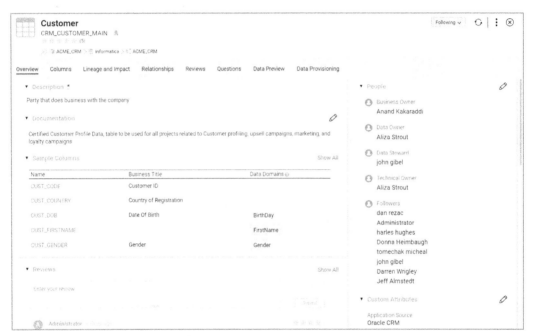

Figure 7-18. Customer table overview screen

The user clicks on the CUST_COUNTRY column name, which brings up the next screen showing the overview for this column, see Figure 7-19. The panel on the right shows information about the table to which this column belongs, including the Application Source, the business description ("Country of Origin"), the business unit ("Sales and Marketing"), and even the load frequency (Weekly).

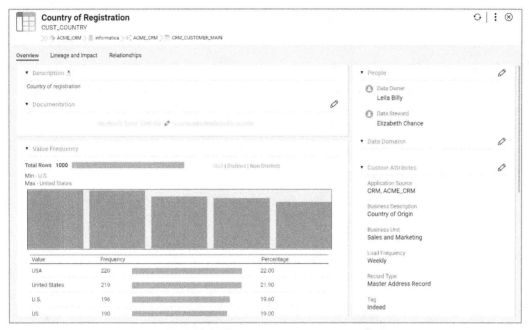

Figure 7-19. Country column overview

The screen in Figure 7-20 provides some profiling details to give a clue as to its data quality (or lack thereof). There are 1000 rows in the table, and the histogram shows that many values are recurring, which is normal. What is not normal are the various ways that the United States has been represented. Based on the minimum and maximum values, it appears that all the records in the table are for Customers in the United States. The highest count value is the string "USA," occurring 220 times. The user scrolls down, revealing more detailed information, shown in Figure 7-20.

Notice all the different ways that the "United States" has been entered into this column, and all of them have fairly high counts, meaning there is no format standardization. This is also revealed in the pattern counts, shown to the right. There are 175 rows with the pattern "X.X.X.," which matches the value "U.S.A." in the histogram pane. The importance to the analyst is that they would have to perform standardization and cleansing on this field to have the values appear in the same format in the resultant data set. The analyst also knows that there is no reason to create a filter for selecting only customers in the United States because there are no international customers in this data set. However, if there were, the analyst would have to cleanse the data and unify it to a single format in order to perform the filter.

Figure 7-20. Column details for data quality inspection

This screen also contains a very helpful pane called "Similar Columns." This helps in Reference Data Management discussed above, to facilitate discovery of reference data candidates to standardize a value like Country across the entire enterprise. It also helps the analyst locate potential data sets to join with their data that might have descriptive information to enrich their final study.

Data quality visualization

IBM provides visualizations without having to leave the catalog environment. Figure 7-21 shows a different data set with many diverse countries. The pie chart helps to visualize which countries have the most entries.

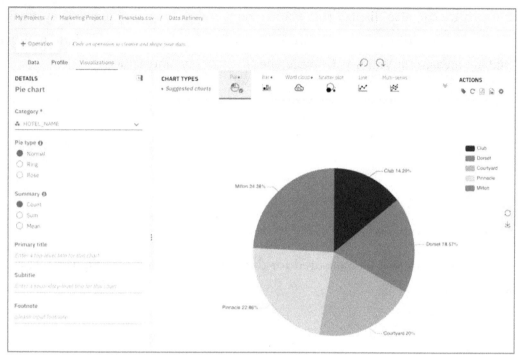

Figure 7-21. Visualization inside the catalog

Data quality rule enforcement

You can perform data quality enforcement with rules and display them and their statuses in the data catalog. Figure 7-22 shows the status of automated rules in Informatica. The red, yellow, and green help to pinpoint potential problems.

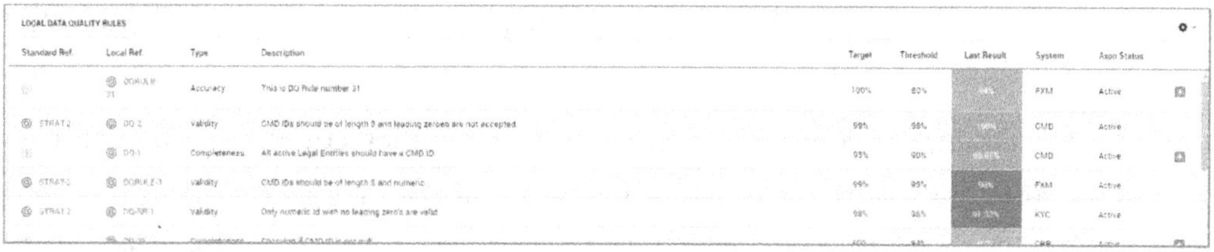

Figure 7-22. Rule status in Informatica

Informatica can also display rule enforcement and data quality levels in systems and business processes. See Figure 7-23. Notice the dimensions of data quality that are measured: Validity, Completeness, Accuracy, and Timely.

Figure 7-23. Rule enforcement and quality levels

Data quality can also be measured for data assets over time, see Figure 7-24 for an example.

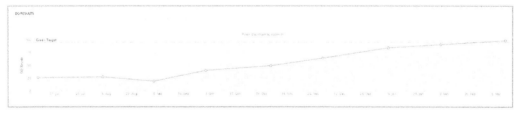

Figure 7-24. Data quality over time

Policies and rules

Policies are laws, regulations, and corporate mandates dictating the proper handling of data. IBM provides a hierarchical structure of Policies, meaning that Policies can have Sub-Policies. Rules can be associated with Policies, adding the actual enforcement of the Policy. An example of a Policy could be that customer addresses must be valid and must be in the same country as stated in the field titled "Country of Residence." There could be two rules that enforce this policy: One that calls address-validation software, and a specialized rule that matches the Customer Country field with the Country of Residence in another data set. Figure 7-25 shows the Policy hierarchy in the left pane and the descriptive information. Note that categories can be assigned to Policies, although this one doesn't have any categories. This policy is a draft and is clearly "under construction." Note the Draft status, shown in blue text name to the name. The user can either delete the draft or sent it for approval. The two choices are shown in red at the top right. The hierarchy shows that this Policy will be a larger policy with sub-policies underneath it.

Figure 7-25. IBM policies

Figure 7-26 shows a rule called "Address In-Country," which probably validates the country field described above. It shows that it is performing "automated enforcement" and the 1,366 times when this was done in March 2019. It even shows that the number of enforcements is up 47.36% from last month. It shows that 100% of the data is anonymized and no access is granted. The number of policy enforcements is tracked over time in the chart for the last month.

Figure 7-26. Address in-country rule

Workflow

Both vendors offer complete data governance suites in addition to data quality functionality. IBM uses the RACI Matrix to assign governance roles to assets and workflows. Figure 7-27 shows the request for approval (1), the tracking of progress (2), and the ability to add comments (3). This allows users to add questions, asking for more clarification or providing a rationale for their decisions. One of the roles of data governance is protecting sensitive data. This was discussed in Chapter 5, but for our purposes here, it is pertinent to point out that this is one of the functions offered by the One-Stop Shop integrated catalogs. They provide data profiling to display granular, descriptive technical metadata supplying clues about the contents of the data, but only when allowed and appropriate.

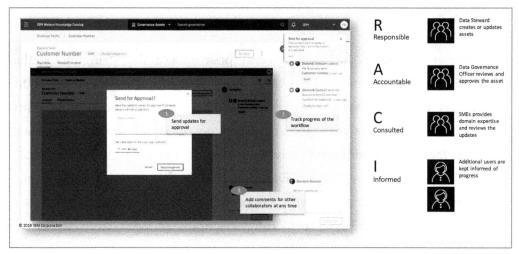

Figure 7-27. RACI governance workflow

Figure 7-28 illustrates a screen from IBM showing a data profile but masking sensitive columns of profiles that are not allowed to be shown. Notice the shields indicating that the profiles for the two columns in the figure are unavailable. The importance of data governance in data catalog implementations was discussed in Chapter 5.

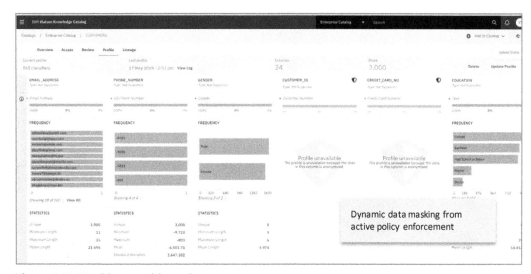

Figure 7-28. Masking sensitive columns

Key points

This chapter focused on the integrated enterprise data catalog, bringing together many different data management capabilities featuring a data catalog at the center. It is important that an enterprise data catalog has functionality in many, if not all the main data management disciplines to enable data management maturity, facilitate curation, and provide trusted data to analysts. Two examples of this kind of catalog are those provided by IBM and Informatica, each offering a vast array of data management components. This chapter highlighted each data management discipline, providing examples of each from these two vendors.

CHAPTER 8

Data Catalog "Add-ons"

My (Bonnie's) adventure with data catalogs started in March 2019 while I was at the Enterprise Data World (EDW) conference, walking the exhibit floor looking for data catalogs for one of my clients. I found a wide variety of data-related products solving various data-related use cases, including data management, data analytics, data governance, and data integration. Some of these products provide metadata management, and when I did a little digging, I discovered that a data catalog offers more than just metadata. This exploration set me off on the journey that had its culmination in this book. I learned that many software products could trace their origins to solving a specific data-related use case. The inventors of these products, during their development, recognized not only the great market demand for data catalogs but that incorporating a catalog component into their base product provided added value. However, often their implementation of catalog functionality misses fundamental features.

Examples of data-related solution providers and product categories we will examine in this chapter are:

- Portal products
- Cloud providers
- Data virtualization and integration
- Business intelligence and data visualization
- Data and process modeling
- Data prep/wrangling
- Service management (APIs and microservices)
- Master Data Management (MDM)

We have labeled these products "add-ons" because they typically provide siloed catalog functionality. They assist the user only in the environment or platform where they reside, thereby limiting their overall usefulness, especially as a data catalog. It should be noted, however, that products change rapidly, and you should always investigate products and the use cases they support when evaluating them. It is also possible that some of these tools may evolve into "stand alone" data catalogs, expanding their functionality into a full-featured product. Another area of growth is in ML-augmentation. This is an important differentiator, discussed in Chapter 10. Many "add-on" catalogs do not have this, and as we will see in Chapter 10 it is critical. A data catalog without it cannot properly perform.

There is a well-understood synergy between data catalogs and overall data management functionality such as data governance. It seems a natural trajectory for a data governance tool, for example, to grow into offering data catalog features. Case in point, that was how Collibra emerged. They first began solving business glossary use cases, offering data governance around glossaries, then made their foray into the catalog arena. However, not every data management or data governance tool qualifies as a data catalog. Some catalog functionality may exist in a product, but a true data catalog covers a wide variety of additional capabilities that may not be included in a data management tool. Certainly, data management platforms can greatly benefit from a catalog, due to the tight coupling of the management to the asset. It can also be said that point solution products solving a single use case can be bolted on to a data catalog by way of APIs. Numerous catalog vendors have been actively engaging partnerships with point solution providers to extend the catalog's functionality: Examples include vendors partnering with Manta for data lineage and Experian Pandora for data profiling.

This chapter also provides us with the opportunity to present other types of data-related products. Space and time did not allow us to include all products that offer an add-on data catalog. A disclaimer as well—the products covered in this chapter have not received the level of detailed research that vendors featured in other chapters have enjoyed. Our knowledge is based on personal experience, industry analysts, white papers, and the Internet. We still felt it was valuable to mention them and point out a few product types that might be of interest.

Portal products: CKAN

There are a few products, mostly open-source, that are portals and not data catalogs. A portal makes resources available and includes simple search features but does not really offer inventory management of data assets.

A portal allows the user to publish and share data. They offer some search capabilities usually through hard-coded web page links but do not have the vast array of metadata that catalogs have. An example of a Portal is CKAN (https://ckan.org/), which is an open-source data portal platform, used by many government entities to provide public access to data based on the Open Data Initiative and other similar data policies and regulations.

A major distinction between a portal and a catalog is the vast array of linkage types that data catalogs provide, such as usage statistics, tying a data asset to users that have either searched for or are actively using the data. Portals don't provide crowdsourcing (unless a programmer manually adds it in). Additionally, portals have very simple metadata. Catalogs on the other hand, provide a rich pool of metadata, along with powerful ML that makes searches smarter the more they are used. Catalogs also provide auto curation and metadata ingest capabilities, automating the inventory collection process.

Cloud providers: Microsoft (Azure)

Each of the major public cloud vendors offer a multiplicity of services that assist data usage. Microsoft Azure offers many services and data storage options, one of which is the Azure Data Catalog. The Azure Data Catalog cuts across all the products and services on the Azure cloud, providing rich metadata about all the data assets stored in Azure. Azure Data Catalog is not available for Azure Stack (the private cloud option) and is also not available for use across other cloud providers. This means that the Azure Data Catalog would not be able to provide services to hybrid cloud or mixed cloud/on-premise environments.

Some independent cloud products (those not offered by the cloud providers themselves) are beginning to support hybrid cloud architectures, but as of this writing, the major cloud providers only offer data catalogs for their own platforms. It should be noted that many of the major data catalog products are branching out and enabling metadata ingest across cloud infrastructures.

Data virtualization and integration tools: Denodo

Data integration tools first emerged as solutions for performing ETL (Extract, Transform and Load) and were used primarily for data warehouses. A second generation of tools were later introduced which enabled users to integrate data virtually; in other words, integrate the data "on the fly" in memory instead of moving it. An example of this type of tool is Denodo.

Denodo has extended its virtualization solution to include data management features. In addition, Denodo and other data integration vendors are offering data catalog add-ons to further enhance their integration functionality. These tools are typically limited by the types of data they can integrate. Most data virtualization tools can handle relational data, but may not be suitable for other forms of data such as document (XML, JSON) and key-value pair. Denodo states that they handle unstructured data, so it's important to verify that all desired data types and formats for your use cases are adequately covered by whatever product you ultimately choose.

Denodo supports cloud environments, which should help improve performance. Historically, data virtualization products had been subject to scalability issues, especially when executing complex joins involving many tables. Data catalogs offered by virtualization vendors may not be able to connect technical metadata with business assets such as processes and glossary. However, our experience with these tools is several years old, and much may have changed in the meantime.

Business intelligence & data visualization tools: Tableau

Many data visualization and Business Intelligence (BI) tools can trace their origins to the start of data warehousing. These tools were used for creating dashboards depicting Key Performance Indicators (KPIs) in attractive visualizations in a single, easy-to-understand screen. They also featured drill-down and rollup capabilities for hierarchical data, such as drill-down sales by a specific region, and then a specific office, and so on. A partial list of these tools is presented here:

- Microsoft Power BI
- Qlik
- Tableau
- MicroStrategy
- Information Builders
- Business Objects
- Cognos

Some of these tools, such as Cognos, were acquired by larger companies (in this case, IBM) and incorporated into their larger product suite offering. The larger suite of products often includes a data catalog function. Others have expanded and have incorporated more and more data management capabilities. One such example is Tableau.

Tableau and Qlik were the first tools to offer superior visualizations while at the same time breaking the cost barrier. Today Tableau markets an analytics platform. Tableau offers a large ecosystem including desktop, server, prep, data management (including governance and catalog), mobile, developer tools, and embedded analytics. The platform is structured around the Tableau universe. The Tableau Catalog description states, "…you get a complete view of all of the data being used by Tableau…"[28] It is a Tableau-centric add-on, limited to Tableau data assets.

Data and process modeling: erwin

erwin Data Modeler (DM) was one of the first Graphical User Interface (GUI) data modeling tools. It evolved from a company called Logic Works, founded in 1993. It was one of the first tools to support IDEF1X and has become ubiquitous in the data modeling community, used by many data modelers through the years. erwin DM also offers an enterprise architecture and business process modeling tool called erwin Evolve. A data modeling tool creates and houses lots of technical metadata, so it is a natural extension of its functionality that it would join with its business process modeling capability and offer a metadata solution. Today, erwin DM's solution includes data governance, data intelligence, data literacy, and data catalog.

---

[28] https://www.tableau.com/products/add-ons/data-management#products.

Many of erwin DM's data catalog strengths are extensions of its data modeling capabilities. For example, the data modeling tool can generate data definition language (DDL) scripts that create database structures consisting of tables, indexes, constraints and other database objects. erwin's data governance and catalog components can generate scripts to perform Master Data Management (MDM), for example. It also leverages its business process component to supply links between business and technical metadata.

Although most of erwin DM's use cases and user base seem to be rooted in the data architect arena and oriented around more technical users, erwin is working on enhancements to their product offering to satisfy more use cases and broaden their market presence to encompass business users as well.

Self-service data prep: Paxata

Paxata is a data prep platform that advocates for democratization of data, empowering data citizens of all user types, including Analysts, Business Leaders, and IT Leaders. It offers exploratory features like interactive data profiling, assisting technical and non-technical users alike in understanding their data. It offers an Embedded Catalog, integrated with its data prep environment, to help users find data and collaborate with each other. Paxata offers the catalog as an add-on to its data prep environment.

API service catalog: Ignite Platform

DigitalML provides an API and microservices management platform supporting the services development lifecycle, including code generation. Their platform includes Holistic Service Catalog which allows service discoverability and categorization, tying services to business functions. DigitalML is not a data or data asset catalog, it only pertains to services. It is possible to host it in addition to a data catalog, but it would be helpful if the data catalog could manage services too, and tie services to data. Some data catalogs can do this, through application objects. Catalogs that contain rich API support can be configured to manage APIs and microservices as either an asset type, application, or function. The ability to manage microservices and tie them to the data they use can be very helpful.

MDM: Reltio

Reltio calls itself a "Modern Master Data Management Platform," providing robust MDM capabilities and customer experiences. An independent industry analyst report[29] stated that in bringing together ML, graph technology, metadata management services, and Big Data, Reltio was providing data catalog functionality. Reltio is oriented toward MDM, and its catalog functionality is in service to that primary goal. MDM by its nature is a heavy metadata activity, so it is not much of a stretch to see that Reltio can be used for data inventory and data management that is broader than just the MDM capability. Reltio's website mentions other areas of data management that it has expanded into, such as data quality, data governance, and workflows. However, Reltio's use case is strongly slanted toward MDM and it may be challenging to expand its usage beyond this scope.

---

[29] Forrester Wave Machine Learning Data Catalogs, 2Q 2018.

Key points

Several vendors are offering creative, useful data management products that provide a data catalog as an enabling technology, but not as their central focus. We have included some examples to introduce and distinguish them from the core data catalog functionality.

Throughout this book, we have explored the realm of data catalogs with the enterprise in mind. One of the biggest gains that a data catalog brings is the ability to make sense of the vast array of enterprise data which includes siloed pockets of dark data that are difficult to find, enabling knowledge of where all the data assets reside. However, there may exist a need for the occasional targeted, siloed use case within the organization that may make a tool with an adjunct data catalog solution appropriate. Examples of this include a standalone data lake with the users focused on data prep, meriting its own prep tool that comes with a data catalog, or a cloud-hosted one by a specific cloud provider.

It should be strongly cautioned that these siloed solutions usually will not scale to become an enterprise data catalog because they either do not have broad functionality or work with all technologies. For example, Azure Data Catalog is not available for Azure Stack, Microsoft's on-premise cloud option. And if you have a hybrid cloud, which utilizes more than one cloud provider, cloud-hosted data catalogs usually will not span across a hybrid environment.

The best solution is to "try before you buy." Create a trial set up in your own environment which the engineers can use. Provide access to not only the toolset offered by the vendor but the tools that the engineers always use. This way, they can test the utility of the vendor tools with their own and see if they are compatible.

CHAPTER 9

Data Lineage

The King Arthur stories and legends tell a tale of the knights going on a quest for the "Holy Grail," the cup that Jesus drank from at the Last Supper before he died. The quest was long and arduous, and the prize was elusive, with no guarantee that it would ever be found, or that it even still existed. Data lineage is like the Grail because it is highly sought after; it has the potential to answer questions like:

- Where did this data come from?
- What is the business purpose for this data? Why was it created?
- Who pushed this data to us?
- When did we get the data?
- Were there any transformations performed on this data? If so, what were they?
- Can I find all the data that is affected by this particular regulation?
- Is the source data for this particular data asset reliable? Is it up-to-date? When was the last load?
- Who is using this data?
- Which reports use this data?
- What data was used to create this BI report?

Data lineage is a hard problem.

Data lineage records the journey that data takes throughout its life in the ecosystem of an organization: from creation or first import to data repositories of various kinds, to reports and dashboards, sometimes to spreadsheets or analytical sandboxes, to models, to data lakes and anywhere else it may reside.

Complete data lineage exposes all the transformations that were performed on the data, and even who or what is using the data, sometimes even exposing queries such as SQL that an analyst may be running. Data lineage is best depicted in diagrams.

It is elusive because all the data catalog products perform it differently.

Lineage benefits

Impact analysis

Lineage relates data assets to others by telling the story around the data flow, including where it came from. It can also show dependencies, such as rules that are the result of policies, and columns that are affected by these rules. Lineage shows the downstream impact of a change. For example, it can answer: How many reports are affected when a column is modified in a table? Indeed, it is especially important for database administrators who have to make a change to the underlying database. Data lineage will help them identify all of the downstream databases, schemas, and reports that will be impacted by the change.

Data set selection

A data analyst needs to understand where the data is coming from in order to determine the suitability of a data set for their particular study. Some data sets are the "source of record"—the original source, such as a Customer Relationship Management (CRM) system which holds and maintains customer master records. The source of record may be data from a transaction processing system or an external data set. But many data sets are derived from other data.

A large percentage of an organization's data is redundant or derived from other data. Data scientists do this often—they get a pertinent data set and extract some data from it, and manipulate it such as changing units of measure to be uniform, especially if they are joining two or more data sets. The resulting data set can be published and made available to other analysts who have similar needs. However, it is important that the lineage (sometimes called provenance) of the data is preserved in the catalog so other analysts know where it came from originally. They can then understand the transformations that were performed on it and whether these are appropriate for their needs. Sometimes, understanding the source of the data may mean that they need to go directly to that source for their study and not use the derivation.

Trust and data quality can also influence the analyst's decision whether to use a specific data source for their analysis, and can also guide decisions for levels of data cleansing to make the data fit for use. Is the source dependable? Data quality measures of source data can answer many questions of suitability and timeliness. Refresh rates can also influence fit for use. A data set that is refreshed only monthly may not meet the needs of the user. The data catalog can also report on deprecated sources, such as a load that did not occur as planned.

Cloud migration

Data lineage can be very helpful when considering which systems should be migrated to the cloud. It can show the data that feeds these systems and strategy can be put in place for how these sources will be handled in the cloud migration. This is also true for the downstream systems of migrated applications.

Compliance

Data lineage is not just for technical metadata. Business metadata can appear in lineage diagrams too, and so can the interaction between technical and business metadata. Business terms can be traced to all the technical assets they describe, such as columns in a database table. Rules can be traced to the policies they enforce. Compliance efforts can determine what data is impacted by policy and verify that the rules are running smoothly.

There are laws and specific regulations that require that the source of certain kinds of data be traceable. Financial data is governed by the Basel Committee on Banking Supervision (BCBS) Rule 239, Principle 2, specifically tracing aggregations (summaries), to ensure that they are accurate. The General Data Protection Regulation (GDPR) sets laws about privacy for European Union (EU) citizens, giving citizens control over their data and the right to be forgotten—to have their data erased. This translates into a data lineage requirement. You have to know where all the data resides for a given person in order to ensure all instances have been erased.

Lineage can also highlight sensitive data that needs to be protected. You can search the catalog for a category, classification, or tag for a specific type of sensitive data and retrieve all the occurrences, then bring up a lineage diagram to determine the data flow and where this data appears.

Lineage capture

"How did the data catalog get the metadata to build the data lineage diagram?"

One vendor stated, "We can only show what our product can see." This is the key. What metadata does each tool have access to? For example, a tool may be able to import metadata from an ETL tool including source to target field mappings but may not be able to see the granular level of each individual transformation.

Several of the vendors we surveyed mentioned that they are actively engaged in partnerships with other vendors that specialize in lineage. For example, Manta is a tool that crunches programming code, deciphering data lineage and feeding it back to the catalog, facilitating the mapping of technical metadata to business terms.[30]

Some vendors obtain lineage from data source-type connectors. Several vendors mentioned that they provide connectors for certain data products that help supply the metadata to provide lineage, for example, ETL tools like Informatica Power Center and IBM DataStage. One vendor mentioned that they used Meta Integration Technology (MITI) connectors but found that they were not robust enough, so they now write their own.

Some vendors such as Alation supply APIs that allow the user to extend the catalog. Alation has a special API for data lineage, see Figure 9-1.

Most vendors that supply query builder and data prep/wrangling tools also provide data lineage from their tools. It is easy because they are naturally collecting the metadata themselves by providing the environment to build these queries.

We can begin to understand the complexity of the problem by looking at types of lineage. Not all tools support all lineage types.

---

[30] https://getmanta.com/.

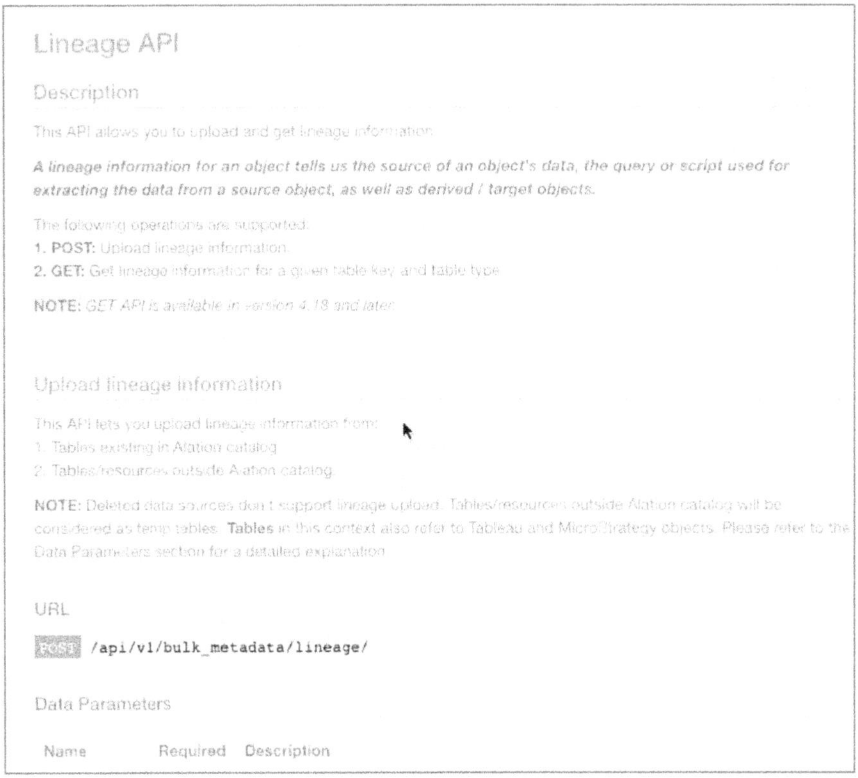

Figure 9-1. Alation's Lineage API

Lineage challenge[31]

The reason why lineage is so difficult to capture and convey in an understandable way is its diversity. The data warehouse is usually populated using one ETL tool. The use of only one vendor enabled metadata management to be simpler, and the ETL vendors were able to provide clear lineage diagrams with drill down into each transformation.

---

[31] The authors are grateful for Alex Gorelik's insightful discussion of Lineage (provenance) in his book *The Enterprise Big Data Lake*, pages 105-110. We based our description of the problem on this section in his book.

Today, many tools are used, and many different varieties of data sources are used. The lineage challenge is two-fold: identification of the systems involved and a look inside the transformation logic that is performed. Data travels through many different systems; it is not just single source and target. Different types of tools are also used to perform the extracts and transformations, for example:

- Traditional ETL jobs expressed visually
- Open source utilities like Sqoop for Hadoop, executing freeform query
- Data wrangling and prep tools
- Programs and code such as Python or R
- Scripts, query languages (SQL scripts)

Add to this complexity different ways of accessing a database such as Java Database Connectivity (JDBC) and Open Database Connectivity (ODBC). Also programming languages like R have their own pseudo-SQL to access relational databases. It may be difficult to decipher that two diverse database accesses are against the same system. It may also be difficult to obtain the columns and transformation logic from all the different types of access methods used. If a freeform query was used, it must be parsed to determine the source(s) and filter and/or transformation logic. Different types of code are used: procedural versus declarative. This further adds to the complexity of the parsing job.

The challenge is further complicated in terms of how the filters, joins, and transformations should be displayed. If the source code is freeform text, should it be further parsed? How should transformations be shown in a visual diagram for code that is not visual? Standard ETL tools would show a transformation as a shape in between the source and target fields, and the user can click on it to see the logic as a symbol representing the function used, further enhancing the graphical representation. If the source transformation is a code and not a symbol, how should this be shown visually? Some tools enable the user to click on the line in the lineage diagram and the code as it is written is shown. However, this is only suitable for more technical users. This drives home the challenge of how to represent transformation, join, and filter logic in a standard way in a lineage series consisting of different source types and technologies.

Lineage categories

We have introduced some of the complexities involved in expressing data lineage. This next section dives into some common types of lineage and how the various tools display each type.

Source to target mappings

The most common data lineage is source to target mappings, and lineage diagrams have been produced by most ETL tools for many years. This is because they "own" their own metadata. The ETL tool was used to create the mappings and transformations, so the tool can easily produce lineage reports. Therefore, it is natural that ETL vendors like Informatica, IBM DataStage, and ab Initio would be able to create lineage diagrams.

Many catalog products display data set level lineage. That is, one data set is used to create a temporary table, which in turn is used to create another table. ETL products can allow the user to drill down to the column level showing column to column mapping. See Figure 9-2 from Informatica. Some catalog products enable you to expand the lineage and give you more visibility into what is happening. The figure shows sliders used to adjust the detail shown in the diagram. Notice the "Tableau" dotted line box in the diagram. This means that CLAIRE was able to infer that the output of the data lake was going to the Tableau report.

Figure 9-2. Data lineage expansion, column to column mapping from Informatica

ETL tools use symbols to indicate the type of transformation, join, or filter that is being used in the lineage. See Figure 9-3 from Informatica. This figure shows the three types being applied with icons. First, the join, then the filter (with a funnel icon), last the function with the mathematical symbol for a function (fx). The join properties are shown in the description box below the lineage diagram, and the logic is shown in the join condition. Although two diagrams from Informatica are from its enterprise data catalog product and not Power Center which is its ETL offering, there is a tight integration between the two.

Figure 9-3. Three types of logic

Figure 9-4 from IBM shows source to target lineage, and users can chat about it. They can ask questions and get clarification from the data steward and/or other users.

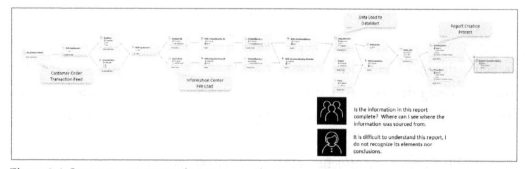

Figure 9-4. Source to target mapping user questions

Query logs

Alation "scrapes" query logs to discover who is using what, down to the query level. Their catalog shows lineage from data sources to queries. The most recent release features column-level lineage from queries.

The screenshot from Alation in Figure 9-5 shows two temporary tables that were created to construct the reports. Note that showing temporary tables in lineage diagrams and consumer tables are options that the user can show or hide as desired, as seen in the box on the screen's bottom left. There are two check boxes provided for these selections.

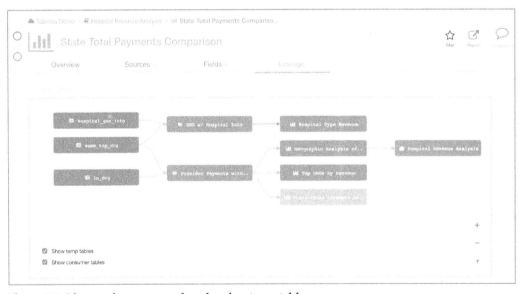

Figure 9-5. Lineage from a query log showing temp tables

The administrator in Alation can perform impact analysis for a data source that is being decommissioned and can set a "Trust Flag" to warn users that the source is being deprecated. TrustCheck can also be automated through an API, such as to indicate a load failure. See Figure 9-6, which shows a problem with the item_price field, and the issue can be traced through the lineage to the FACT_TBL_SUMM and affecting other fields along the way.

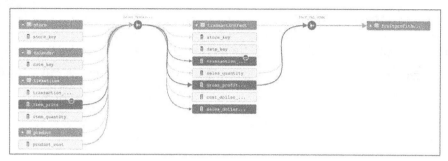

Figure 9-6. Deprecated field propagated in lineage

SQL scripts

Some tools like Informatica can parse hand-coded SQL scripts to decipher column-level data flows and the transformations used. Others are using third party tools such as Manta to perform this function. Figure 9-7 from Informatica shows the internals for a HiveQL script.

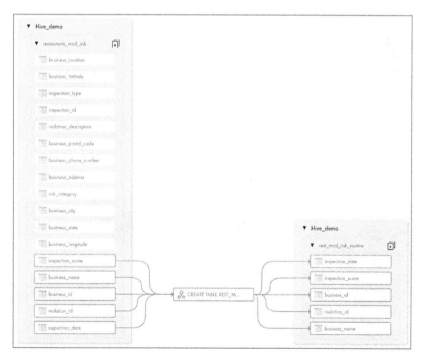

Figure 9-7. HiveQL lineage

Business processes

Data lineage can be used to explain the business processes behind how the data was created. See Figure 9-8 from Informatica. This diagram maps out a business process that is used to detect customer sentiment. When a degradation is detected, a rule is fired which presents the customer with an offer, and tracks the customer's response.

Figure 9-8. Business process lineage

Business to technical metadata mappings

Many products such as Collibra can trace business metadata to technical assets. Figure 9-9 shows the summary page for a specific data set called Customer Product Sales Data. The Summary page shows the Business Context for this asset, and ties it to data models and business glossary items.

The user clicks on the "Diagram" in the menu on the left of the screen and arrives at a data lineage diagram, see Figure 9-10. This diagram shows what system the data comes from and which Tableau reports are using it.

Figure 9-9. Collibra summary page

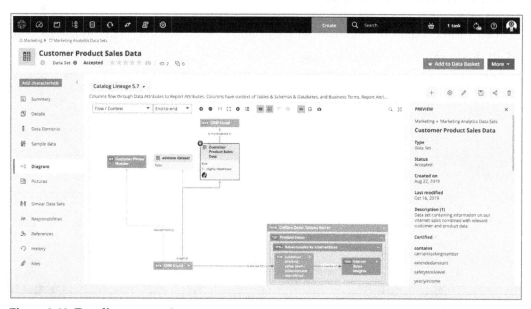

Figure 9-10. Data lineage step 1

The user can drill down further to see how the physical data assets are related to business data domains, as shown in Figure 9-11. Note that Figure 9-11 displays the legend explaining the colors and symbols on the diagram.

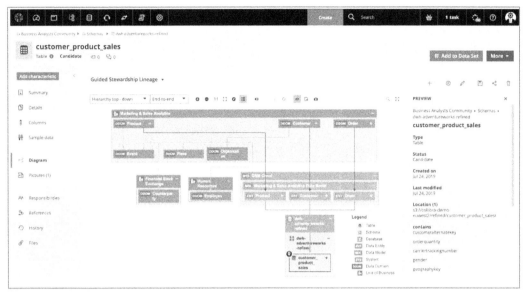

Figure 9-11. Drill down to data domain connections

An end-to-end data flow can be seen in Figure 9-12. You can click on the lines to drill down into transformation logic.

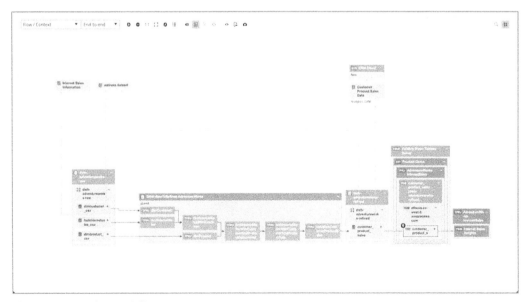

Figure 9-12. End-to-end flow

Collibra populates its lineage from integration with supported sources such as ETL tools and AWS Glue Data Catalog. It also works with Manta, which expands the number of lineage sources that Collibra can support.

Business policy to rules

Lineage can also show the ties between business-oriented assets like policies and regulations and data sets. A user looking at the screen from Collibra in Figure 9-13 sees a GDPR standard of a 12-month retention period. Using the diagram, he can tell which data sets, the boxes in yellow, comply with this standard. He can also see that the standard is a retention period because it is attached to a retention policy.

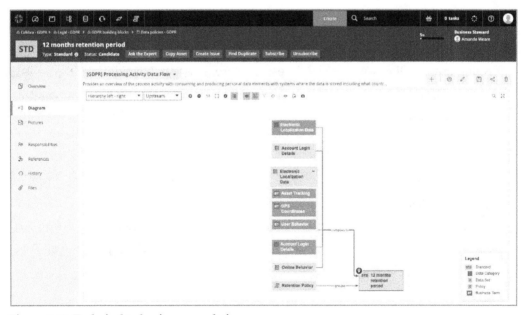

Figure 9-13. Technical to business regulation

Figure 9-14 from Informatica shows a technical lineage, including the results of a user selecting the "Show Business Terms" icon at the top right. Figure 9-14 shows the business terms along with each table name.

Figure 9-14. Business terms in technical lineage

Relationship diagrams

Some data catalog tools allow the user to map all sorts of relationships by way of Relationship Diagrams, which in essence are a type of lineage; see Figure 9-15 for an example of a high-level relationship diagram from Informatica. Knowledge graphs, to be defined in the next chapter, make these relationships possible.

Figure 9-15 shows all of the various associations to a data asset called CRM_CUSTOMER_MAIN. This is probably the Customer Master, the source of record for all customers in the organization. Key components are business glossary terms, which help to define the business context of data assets. Note the legend at the top right, which enables the user to show or hide the asset types desired.

Figure 9-16 shows a relationship diagram from Collibra, showing the various asset types related to the ABC Data Assets Part data set, including database columns, a report, business terms, and a relationship from a business term to a column.

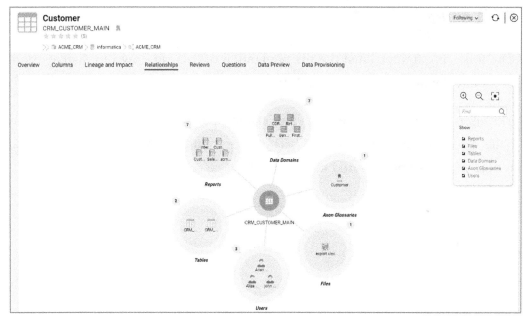

Figure 9-15. High-level relationship diagram

Figure 9-16. Collibra relationship diagram

Drill down

The following figures illustrate the navigation of drilling down to display more and more details of a data flow in Informatica.

The user first examines the overview catalog page for a Tableau report called Sales Revenue, seen in Figure 9-17. The page contains a picture from the actual report which can be included using an API.

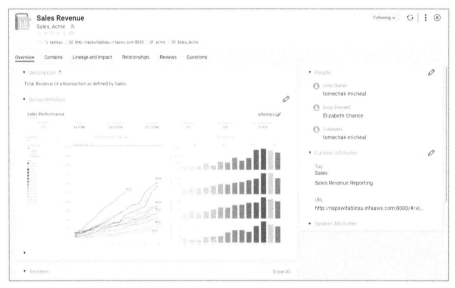

Figure 9-17. Overview page for a report

Next, the user clicks on the Lineage and Impact tab, which brings up the lineage diagram shown in Figure 9-18. It shows the various tables that are used to create the Tableau report. Note the sliders at the top, which can be used to expand the detail displayed in the diagram.

The user would like to see more details, especially how the tables relate to each other, so the slider is used to show this, which is reflected in Figure 9-19.

Figure 9-18. Table lineage for the report

Figure 9-19. More detailed table lineage

The user would like to see column-level lineage and clicks on the first icon at the top, which displays circles next to tables containing logic shown in Figure 9-20.

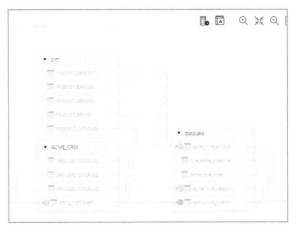

Figure 9-20. Drilling down within a table

Clicking on the circle within ACME_CRM for CRM_CUSTOMER brings up the expanded Hive lineage shown in Figure 9-21.

Figure 9-21. Hive lineage

Figure 9-22 shows a function performing a calculation. Column lineage can be obtained, and a select box appears, allowing the user to select which columns they would like to see, as shown in Figure 9-22.

The result of the selection is shown in Figure 9-23. Hovering over the icon shows the actual logic performed. Figure 9-23 shows the email address being constructed by concatenating the first name and last name separated by a period, concatenating the @ sign and the string "informatica.com." (What happens if there's two people with the same name?!)

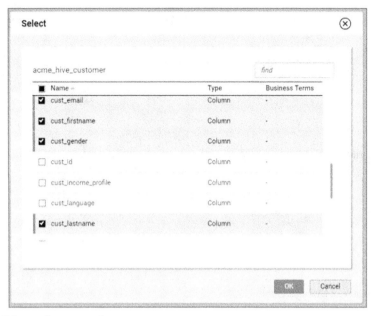

Figure 9-22. Select columns to show

Figure 9-23. Column-level lineage

Inferred lineage

ML can be used to infer lineage from the data assets in the catalog. Waterline uses "fingerprinting" to store many different properties about all data assets, as we discussed in Chapter 6. Waterline can leverage the fingerprints and propose the sources that are most likely to be the actual sources, see Figure 9-24. Notice that a box will show a description of the inferred lineage with the option to reject it if necessary.

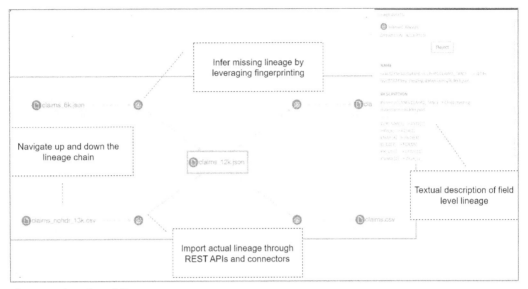

Figure 9-24. Inferred lineage

Key points

This chapter illustrated many different kinds of data lineage that data catalogs can display. Lineage allows you to trace a data asset's original source and all the hops along the way. It can trace data that are affected by rules and policies. It can enable the user to scrutinize the sources of the data to determine if they are trustworthy. We saw in Chapter 5 the importance of tracing business purpose to data for regulatory compliance.

Make sure you ask the vendor to demonstrate data lineage and how it works when considering the purchase of a specific data catalog product. The vendors differ greatly in this functionality. Here's a summary of some of the data lineage types:

- Business glossary term to database columns
- Policies/regulations and data affected

- Source to target mappings such as those used in a data warehouse
- Data sources to BI reports
- Database tables to data lake
- Raw files to data lake
- Data sources used in a query
- Queries used in a report
- Data steward to resources managed
- Logical/Enterprise model Critical Data Elements (CDE) to physical data
- Scripts to tables, columns, and other technical assets
- Policies to rules that enforce the policies
- Business processes that are the source for data
- Sources and lineage of sensitive data

## CHAPTER 10

Machine Learning in the Data Catalog

We have discussed throughout this book how the data glut is causing more and more organizations to look for an automated solution to managing its distributed and diverse data sprawl. A ML-powered data catalog provides a solution that is scalable and facilitates data management, and also enables data citizens of all expertise levels to be more productive with data.

This chapter takes an inside look into what ML provides and its important role in the data catalog solution. Although some of the concepts in this chapter have been introduced before, here we bring together the mechanics, the value of ML and the central role it plays in data catalogs.

Industry analysts[32] have pointed out that inventorying data is one of the biggest challenges many organizations face. The Foundations for Evidence-Based Policymaking Act of 2018 (hereafter referred to as the "Evidence Act") mandates in Title II, Open Government Data Act that:

Each agency shall develop and maintain a comprehensive data inventory *and designate a Chief Data Officer.* [33] (emphasis added)

We have discussed how manually creating an inventory is impossible in today's data flood. The only way to do this is by leveraging AI and ML technology to help. Gartner Group states:

---

[32] Most notably Gartner, in "Augmented Data Catalogs: Now an Enterprise Must-Have for Data and Analytics Leaders", 12 September 2019, p.2.

[33] https://www.congress.gov/bill/115th-congress/house-bill/4174.

> *By 2022, over 60% of traditional IT-led data catalog projects that do not use ML to assist in finding and inventorying data distributed across a hybrid/multicloud ecosystem will fail to be delivered on time, leading to derailed data management, analytics and data science projects.*[34]

Gartner is calling out the hybrid or multicloud ecosystem, but the observation can apply to all environments, even those that have not yet moved to the cloud. Everyone is swimming in data and some level of automation is absolutely required to manage the flood.

ML to the rescue

We defined ML in chapter 1 as "…an application of Artificial Intelligence (AI) that provides systems the ability to automatically learn and improve from experience without being explicitly programmed."[35] *Artificial Intelligence* is defined by Oxford Dictionaries as:

> *The theory and development of computer systems able to perform tasks normally requiring human intelligence, such as visual perception, speech recognition, decision-making, and translation between languages.*[36]

AI and ML as applied to the data catalog technology mean that the software can make inferences and create new knowledge from existing knowledge that is in the catalog. It can organize the knowledge in such a way as to enable the

---

[34] Gartner, Ibid., p. 2.

[35] http://www.expertsystems.com.

[36] https://www.lexico.com/en/definition/artificial_intelligence.

creation of new insights and business context. It can relate assets in the catalog to other assets. The more that users interact with it, the more the system "learns" and adds to its knowledgebase. It is a great and practical application of ML, enabling faster time to insight, making data scientists, data stewards, and data consumers more productive.

The good news is, ML has matured as a discipline, and so has the ML capability within the data catalog. Today's data catalog needs ML. ML simplifies and enhances the following areas of data usage:

- Automate Ingest & Enrich
  - o Automate data ingestion
  - o Create semantic relationships (tie business concepts, glossary terms, and tags to data)
  - o Recognize secure/protected data and handle it appropriately
  - o Run rules on data tagged from recommendations
  - o Run and use profiles to recognize semantic concepts

- Simplify search and discovery
  - o Recommend resources based on many factors such as related assets or prior searches
  - o Understand and infer business context behind the search terms and return relevant resources
  - o Understand natural language phrases used in searches

- Facilitate data and metadata governance
  - o Track data lineage
  - o Utilize crowdsourcing to aid in governance
  - o Enable policy and rule enforcement
  - o Anomaly detection

- Provision
  - o Assist in query building and recommending

o   Suggest data sets that can be used together

o   Discover duplicate data sets

o   Facilitate query reuse

Figure 10-1 from Informatica illustrates some of these points.

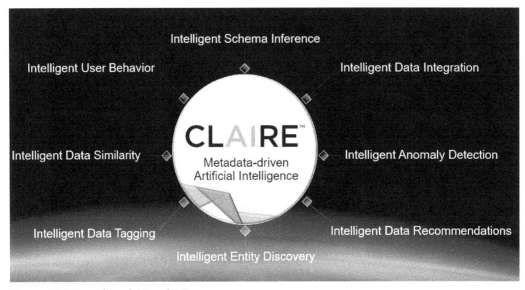

Figure 10-1. Benefits of AI and ML

ML and the data catalog

We introduced the reader in Chapter 1 to the concept that data catalogs provide two major functions:

- Curation
- Intelligent search

Data must come in quickly and efficiently, be classified, and determined what it means and how it fits with all the other body of knowledge, so it can be found easily and used appropriately. We will discuss these major topics and how ML is essential to both. At the heart of enabling both is the ability to make associations.

Knowledge graph

The fundamental task of ML is to intelligently make associations of all kinds, to enable quick and efficient ingest of new data, and to enable intelligent search.

One way ML works is to use a graph, called a *Knowledge graph*, to store internal connections between facts and to associate many kinds of data assets and metadata. We introduced this concept in the last chapter on data lineage. It is central to the ML operation. Here is an easy to understand definition:

> *A knowledge graph is a programmatic way to model a knowledge domain with the help of subject-matter experts, data interlinking, and machine learning algorithms.*[37]

Figure 10-2 from Informatica shows a conceptual rendering of various types of data assets related in the knowledge graph to one particular data asset. Many data catalogs use such a graph, usually implemented in a graph data store. Its utility is in its ability to link many diverse types of data and metadata together, so even seemingly unlikely connections can be found. This is the main source of power of ML—it learns from connections that already exist and infers new connections from them.

---

[37] https://bit.ly/3134Em1.

Figure 10-2. Knowledge graph from Informatica

Many such knowledge graphs are maintained in the catalog, containing clusters of related data assets. See Figure 10-3, again from Informatica.

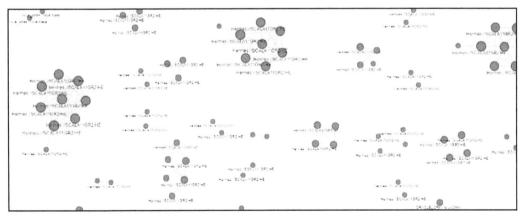

Figure 10-3. Clusters of knowledge graphs

Waterline's Fingerprint Library is the foundation for all the connections that can be made between the diversity of data assets. Figure 10-4 shows that the discovery platform can infer auto tags, joins, lineage, duplicates (copies of data, data redundancy), and apply tag-based rules. The Aristotle Classification Engine can use the fingerprint library to make predictions.

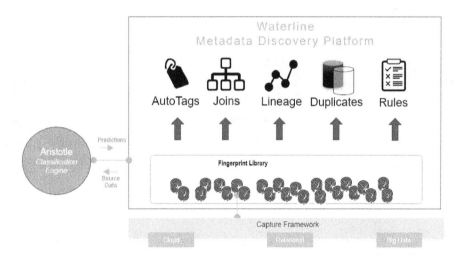

Figure 10-4. Fingerprinting and connections

Similarity

Similarity is the process of discovering and presenting assets that are alike and could potentially be duplicates. It is yet another association that ML provides and can help a data analyst select a data set other than the one they are viewing in the catalog. Perhaps the data set under review is not quite right but something similar could be better suited. Informatica's CLAIRE looks for column similarity based on data overlap of several factors that are tunable relative to each other. It uses Jaccard Coefficient and Bray Curtis Similarity. It can be compared with the photo tagging you see in some social media sites, see Figure 10-5.

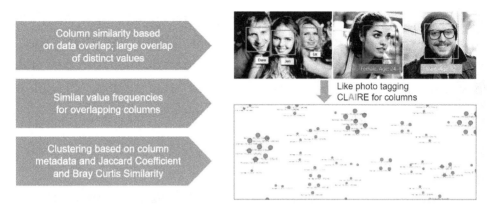

Figure 10-5. Similarity compared with photo tagging

Similar columns are determined by unsupervised clustering based on names, unique values, and patterns observed in the data. There is an overall similarity score computed for each pair factored with the three similarity type weights. Users can modify the weights that each type contributes to the overall score. See Figure 10-6.

Figure 10-6. Column similarity in Informatica

Notice in Figure 10-6 that Cust_Country was compared to three other columns that showed a high degree of similarity. The highest factor for each was the distinct values (the largest bar in each).

Figure 10-7 shows a more nuanced example comparing columns to Origin_Airport. Airport codes are interesting reference data because there are three standards groups that maintain similar sets of codes:

- International Air Transport Association (IATA)
- Federal Aviation Administration (FAA)
- International Civil Aviation Organization (ICAO)

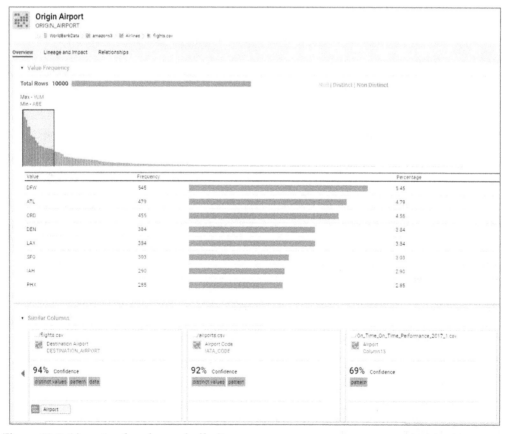

Figure 10-7. Airport code column similarity

This means that airport codes, though semantically equivalent (each data set contains codes that designate airports), their values may differ—the code sets sometimes contain different codes for the same airport. Sometimes the values overlap. For example, the FAA maintains codes only for airports in the US, and their codes sometimes overlap with one or both of the other two sets. This probably explains why there's a lower similarity score for one of the columns in Figure 10-7. It is probably a different code set, but still the same data semantically.

IBM's Watson also enables the user to select various matching methods for specific data classes and columns. Figure 10-8 shows the various methods from which a user can choose.

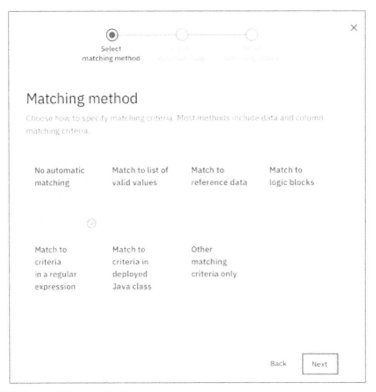

Figure 10-8. IBM's matching methods

ML and the human

Chapter 6 discussed the effect that the influx of large quantities and diverse varieties of data into the enterprise is having and the lack of ability to manage all the data manually. Data management is the discipline that makes sense of data and ensures that it is fit for use. Traditional methods of data management and data governance cannot keep up with the data flood. Data management is definitely needed along with a data asset inventory so it can be understood. Therefore, one of the most important roles of ML is to apply automation and algorithms which add context and business meaning to data so that humans can use it—and to do this by involving humans less and less.

Chapter 6 outlined the importance of the partnership between human and ML. Curation is the human's role in the process, approving and rejecting the recommendations ML makes. ML relies heavily on human participation to hone its knowledge. Certainly, when a data catalog is first deployed, there is a large human investment upfront. This investment can be mitigated by the import of various business artifacts such as business glossaries and data dictionaries, which establish a baseline from which the data catalog can first be used.

There are many ways that the user contributes to this knowledgebase. In fact, even the searches that the user enters in the catalog are used to build its knowledge. It learns the user's likely searches and can link these assets to other related assets and recommend those that the user might be interested in. It can also gain knowledge about how data relates to other data from these searches and can use this intelligence to make recommendations to others when they perform similar searches. Figure 10-9 shows data assets that Watson recommends. Notice that Highly Rated and Recently Added assets are also made available.

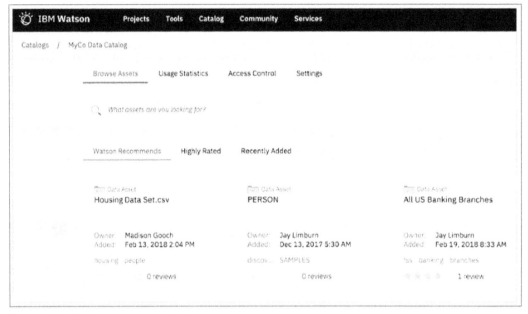

Figure 10-9. Watson recommended assets

Interestingly, as we see in the discussion above, curation involves not only the data steward. The data steward and data governance processes perform certification of data assets and oversee data quality, so they play a big role in curation, but all users contribute to the knowledgebase.

Figure 10-10 from Informatica shows some of the ways that humans add information into the catalog, and the catalog gains from the human interactions of reviews, ratings, questions/answers, data set certifications, and business term associations.

The data steward can check on how the recommender engine is doing by searching for all assets with a specific tag. The search will reveal the assets showing the confidence level. The data steward can drill down and see details of a specific field and then accept or reject the tag. See Figure 10-11 from Waterline.

Figure 10-10. Human and ML interaction

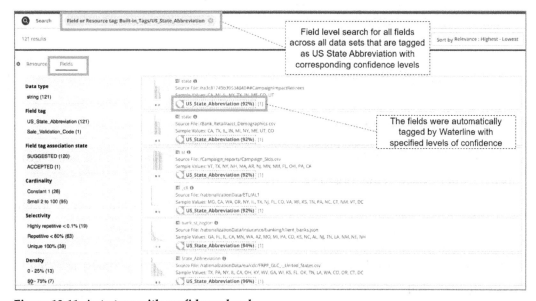

Figure 10-11. Auto tags with confidence level

Intelligent semantic search

ML builds and uses context, coming from the glossary as well as the user's past searches, as explained above. Figure 10-12 from Informatica shows a user's search on the term "grade," and ML suggests assets having something to do with "tier." A different recommendation would be made if the organization was a college or university. "Grade" would instead bring up different connections such as "score," "exam," or "GPA."

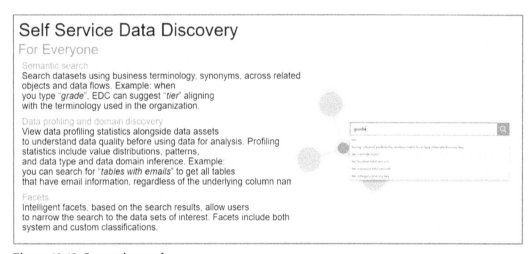

Figure 10-12. Semantic search

Watson looks for semantically similar concepts in unstructured data, see Figure 10-13, which shows the business concepts found in a study by J.D. Power concerning Auto Claims. Watson sees that it is related to Insurance, even though the word "Insurance" does not appear in the name or description.

Unifi recognizes natural language sentences the user can type, such as, "Show me data sets that…." Clicking on the lightbulb icon brings up suggestions of natural language sentences that can be used, see Figure 10-14.

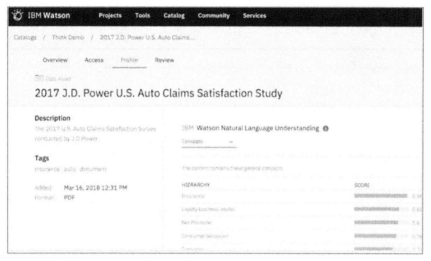

Figure 10-13. Natural language understanding

Things to try		
Metadata	**Column Stats**	**Dataset Stats**
what is the description of <column>	what is the average of <dataset|column>	what is the row count of <dataset>
show me the metadata of <column>	show me the stats for <dataset|column>	what is the column count of <dataset>
show me the md of <column>	show me min, max and count of <dataset|column> <dataset|column>	what is the size of dataset <dataset>

Figure 10-14. Unifi's natural language suggestions

Domains

A Domain in Informatica is a business category, which together with other domains form a business information model or conceptual data model. Domains can contain other domains, such as shown in Figure 10-15. It shows how domains and business concepts are associated with technical metadata.

CLAIRE can recognize the connections and link them automatically. This is a typical use of AI. To the human, this looks obvious, but it takes reasoning and inference, which AI/ML performs well.

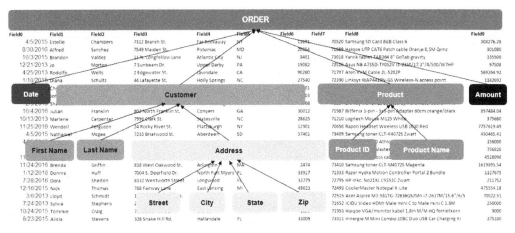

Figure 10-15. Composite domains

Recognizing domains and making connections becomes especially powerful when performed against unstructured data, where domains are recognized from freeform text, as shown in Figure 10-16. Excel, Word, PDF, text files, and PowerPoint files are examples of unstructured data formats that can be supported. Note how these business domains are recognized in the data parsed from a Sherlock Holmes story (to follow our sleuthing theme!).

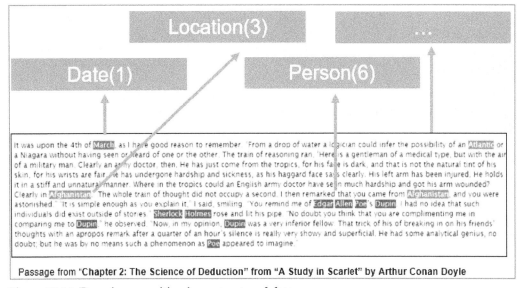

Figure 10-16. Domain recognition in unstructured data

Classifications

Classifications are sensitivity markers in IBM WKC. They assist data stewards to quickly identify assets that require special treatment, such as Personally Identifiable Information (PII) or Personal Health Information (PHI). Users in the federal government are familiar with classifications such as Secret and Top Secret. See Figure 10-17 which shows a data steward searching for classifications.

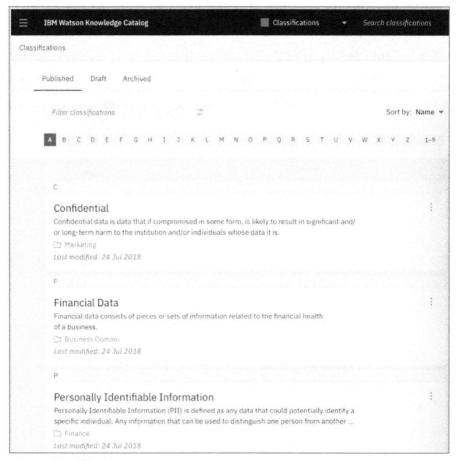

Figure 10-17. Classifications

Chapter 5 covered data governance functionality including privacy and security. Classifications can be inferred and recommended based on rules and similar data/associations. For example, a field that looks like a Social Security Number, following the typical pattern of numbers and hyphens, can be inferred to be PII.

Inferred joins

Watson can recommend data sets that can join together, see Figure 10-18. We saw this demonstrated also in Chapter 6 in Waterline Data's product. This is a huge help to both technical and non-technical users, as bringing together data sets is a big part of the analysis. Often, one data set alone is not enough to answer the question. Determining data sets that can join and the fields that can be used to accomplish the join can be a laborious process. The data catalog can make helpful time-saving recommendations.

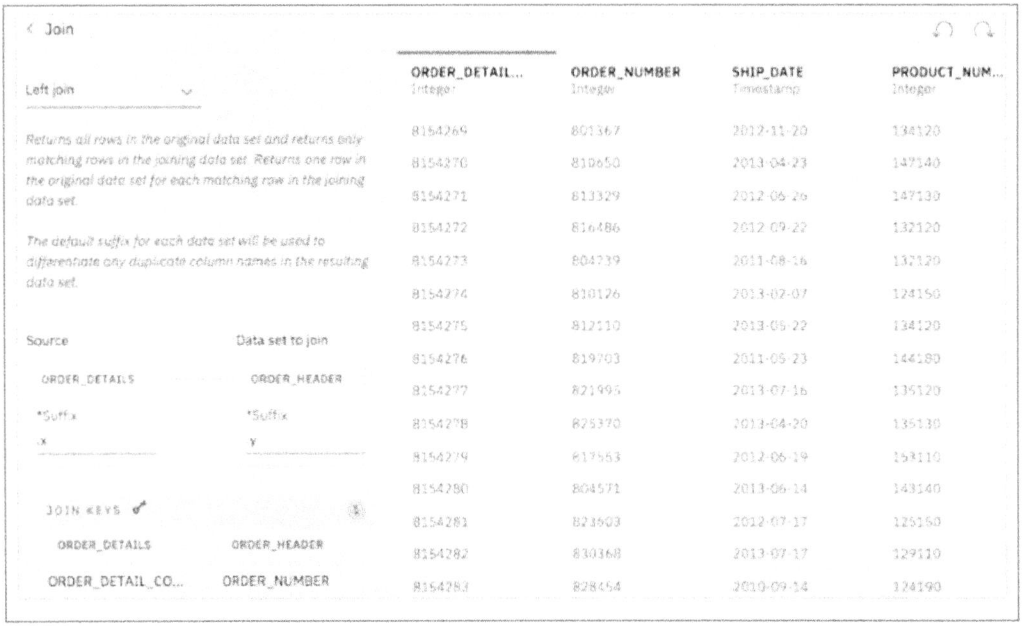

Figure 10-18. Recommended joins

Inferred lineage

Chapter 9 explored data lineage, and how data catalogs can infer data provenance and explain the origins of data, which is mandated by certain regulations such as EU's GDPR. ML crawls through and finds all the uses of data, such as files, staging areas, data warehouses, data marts, and reports. Some products can even infer data lineage from SQL scripts and queries. See Figure 10-19 from Informatica.

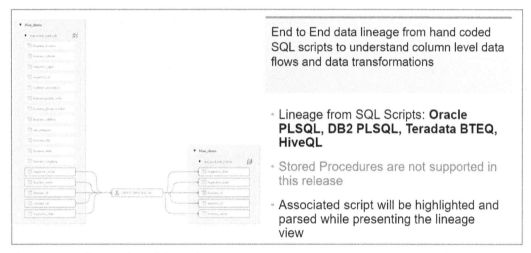

Figure 10-19. Lineage from SQL scripts

Key points

ML is absolutely essential for data catalogs—without it, the data catalog becomes a manual, human-only powered tool. This is what the metadata repositories introduced a decade or so used to provide. Data would be ingested via "scanners" which could be automated, but linkages between metadata types would have to be done manually. The exceptions were "one-stop shop" tools, like those outlined in Chapter 7, but the linkage ability was restricted to only those tools in the suite provided by the one vendor. Common examples were Informatica Power Center and IBM InfoSphere. These products, before the advent of their ML data cataloging capabilities, were not able to accept metadata sources outside of their toolset or did so with great technical acumen and considerable manual effort.

With the pairing of ML and cataloging capability, ML enables intelligent associations to be made at scale, finally providing the ability to keep pace with the data glut. This enables data scientists to be more efficient and provides them with faster speed to insight and enables data self-service to businesspeople. It also empowers data governance personnel and data stewards to actively protect data and keep up with increasing regulatory compliance standards. ML is essential for both intelligent curation and intelligent search.

CHAPTER 11

Data Catalog Features

This chapter contains a summary of all data catalog features. Interestingly, some of our sponsors and clients have asked for a features list when they found out we were writing this book! This feature list will help in several ways:

- If you are in the market for a data catalog, it can help you determine from your use cases which features would be the most beneficial. The feature list can be whittled down to include the most important features for you, and this shortlist can then be used as a rating tool to select the best one that fits these requirements.

- If you already own a catalog, it can help you determine the strengths of your product and its weaknesses. You can then be armed with a list of desired enhancements that you can use to launch a meaningful conversation with your vendor to determine their roadmap and potentially propose improvements.

- If you are considering whether a catalog is the next step for your environment, use this list to see how a catalog can benefit you.

One way you can use the Features List is to capture your use cases, then map each to the features that enable the use case. The categories are oriented around function so they can be mapped easily to use cases. You can download the list from the book's webpage at https://technicspub.com/TheDataCatalog/. You can then customize it specifically for your purposes. Excel is a wonderful tool. You can create scoring spreadsheets with formulas in the summary page which take all the cells from all individual pages, adding and averaging them together.

Feature categories

This chapter brings together all the features we have introduced throughout the book and organizes them into 19 categories. Some features may be able to fit in more than one category, an example of this is "ML assistance when entering search text," which we have classified in the Search and Use category, but it could just as easily fit under Machine Learning. We have done our best to choose what we feel is the best match when encountering these situations.

We have resisted the temptation to list a feature more than once. However, there are a few features in the list that can be seen as potential duplicates but they have a nuance that may distinguish them slightly, for example, there may be some overlap between features listed in the Search & Use category and the Data Asset Page Appearance. Feel free to move any feature in your copy around if you believe a different category suits it better. The 19 categories with brief descriptions are listed in Table 11-1.

Table 11-1. Data Catalog Feature Categories

Category Name	Description
Machine Learning (ML)	The application of machine learning in catalog functions, especially similarity and semantic clustering.
Automated Discovery & Capture	Features surrounding the automation of ingesting metadata and discovery of new or changed assets.
Metadata Capture	Features concerning the types of metadata and the mechanics of metadata capture.
Search & Use	The mechanics of searching in the catalog and using the search results.
Data Asset Page Appearance	The layout, look and feel of the asset pages in the catalog and the ability to understand the metadata presented.
Curation and Tagging	Features that facilitate curation, the human assisting the ML to increase catalog knowledge and make assets more discoverable. This category includes the ability to tag and governance around tagging.

Category Name	Description
Collaboration and Crowdsourcing	The collection of features that enable users to communicate with each other and to collaborate concerning data within the catalog. This includes rating data sources and annotations.
Vendor Quality & Roadmap	Features that measure how easy the vendor is to deal with, how their roadmap corresponds to your list of priority features and how responsive they are.
Extensibility	The ability to extend the catalog and customize it, adding metadata types and new fields, and designing asset pages. It also deals with getting data out of the catalog and into other systems.
Metadata Attributes	List of general metadata properties that can be included in a data catalog.
Data Governance	The support of protecting, monitoring and administering data assets through formal oversight. Includes privacy and risk.
Business Glossary	The support of a business glossary and its ongoing governance and maintenance, with the ability to associate business terms with all other data assets.
Data Quality	The ability to measure, control and report on data quality of data assets.
Data Profiling	Descriptive statistics on each column in a table; contains min, max, #/% nulls, #/% unique values, value and pattern frequency distribution, etc.
Data Lineage	The tracing of related data assets usually in the form of a lineage diagram.
Architecture/ Administration/ Infrastructure/ Security	The tool's administrative functions including setting permissions and monitoring performance. Also includes architecture and infrastructure considerations including platform.
Data Preparation	The support of query building including joins, filtering and functions. Can include job administration and monitoring.
Business Domains and Processes	Support for business conceptual model and business processes, associating them to other asset types especially technical physical data and rules.
Data Analyst Tool/Big Data Integration	Integration with data scientist tools and environments at scale.

Data catalog features

The Features are shown in Table 11-2 by category. We have numbered them also by category for easy reference.

Table 11-2. Data Catalog Features List

#	Feature
1.00	**Machine Learning (ML)**
1.01	Uses ML to augment the catalog
1.02	Uses graphs for asset associations
1.03	Recognizes similar data sets and suggests duplicates
1.04	Offers ability to tune similarity basis such as name, pattern, values, and establish relative weights for each
1.05	Provides confidence factor reported with auto tag assignment
1.06	Offers thresholds for auto tagging
1.07	Identifies business processes related to data sets or terms
1.08	Provides association algorithms (such as "fingerprinting")
1.09	Performs a file/data set compare such as discovering the same schema across many data sets at once
1.10	Recommends assets based on similar searches, both from current user and similar users
2.00	**Automated Discovery and Capture of Data Assets**
2.01	Crawls for data set auto discovery
2.02	Auto captures all major meta-attributes
2.03	Auto ingests metadata when new source is detected
2.04	Auto tags and catalogs data sets
2.05	Auto updates metadata when source system is updated or changed
2.06	Auto captures sample data
2.07	Auto discovers business term usage and affinity

#	Feature
2.08	Ingests metadata at scale, appropriate to use case
3.00	**Metadata Capture**
3.01	Recognizes and captures diverse data types and formats, such as relational, JSON, and key/value
3.02	Creates format specification rules to be executed upon ingest (can be treated as a data quality expectation)
3.03	Tunes the amount of sample data captured, both for default and for specific data sets
3.04	Turns off the capture of sample data for sensitive data sets
3.05	Ingests data dictionaries
3.06	Ingests conceptual, logical, and physical data models
3.07	Captures data usage information (from query logs or other sources)
3.08	Ingests business glossaries
3.09	Uses a scheduler
4.00	**Search & Use Features**
4.01	Offers all-purpose google-like search bar to search on any asset type, available on any catalog page
4.02	Provides natural language, key word, and faceted searches
4.03	Provides ML-recommended assets based on factors such as tags, glossary, prior searches
4.04	Provides ML recommend certified assets over others and priority in results display
4.05	Searches for PII or sensitive data category/classification
4.06	ML assists when entering search text (such as providing options beginning with characters typed)
4.07	Includes related assets based on semantic similarity through tags and ML associations in search results

#	Feature
4.08	Includes related assets based on others' similar searches in search results
4.09	Allows users to watch a data set (or individual asset), receiving notification of any changes or activity
4.10	Supports both internal and external links, and links to other catalog pages and resources (such as SMEs)
4.11	Allows experienced user to create a parameterized form for less experienced user
4.12	Provides a smart query builder for less technical analysts
4.13	Navigates to other tools such as BI dashboards from the catalog with appropriate credentials and permissions
5.00	**Data Asset Page Appearance**
5.01	Provides easy to understand and comprehensive layout of major asset page
5.02	Provides easy to access related information from main asset page
5.03	Offers drill down to details from any page via intuitive and easy navigation
5.04	Shows Points of Contact (PoCs) on all relevant asset pages
5.05	Shows trustable attributes such as certification, ratings, and data quality on all relevant asset pages
5.06	Displays diverse formats such as JSON in an understandable way (such as translating it into columnar format)
5.07	Indicates the type of asset such as table, column, business object, and report, using an icon in the data asset page and search results
5.08	Shows joined data sets
6.00	**Curation and Tagging**
6.01	Supports manual and automated curation (metadata & tagging)
6.02	Assigns the ability to tag by permission

#	Feature
6.03	Provides the ability to manage tags, delete tags, and monitor usage of tags
6.04	Offers both automated and manual entry and cataloging of data sets
6.05	Supports the ability to add/delete/hide data sets
6.06	Provides user-friendly interface to allow owners and administrators to add, update, and delete entries
6.07	Provides reporting features and related customization
6.08	Supports business, technical and operational tags
7.00	**Collaboration and Crowdsourcing**
7.01	Supports collaboration features to enable and capture user annotations, comments, descriptions and sharing
7.02	Supports crowdsourced metadata and enables subject matter experts to tag and describe data
7.03	Allows users to rate (like, star rating) data sets for accuracy, completeness, usefulness
7.04	Allows users to write reviews of data sets
7.05	Provides Wiki-like editing of descriptive metadata
7.06	Supports personalization features for users to personalize settings, create alerts on tags, and so on
7.07	Displays answers to questions users can ask of SMEs and/or data stewards and/or other users
7.08	Recognizes the role of the user so users can see the input of stewards' knowledge to increase trust
7.09	Provides chat facility enabling users to carry on conversations regarding a data asset
7.10	Offers the ability to watch a data set and be notified if there's any changes or activity
8.00	**Vendor Quality/Roadmap**

#	Feature
8.01	Supports relevant and important features and enhancements including interoperability with other tools and applications as required
8.02	Provides frequent releases and major versus minor releases per period
8.03	Includes high quality documentation
8.04	Includes quality and responsive technical support
8.05	Onboarding complexity and onboarding vendor support
8.06	Provides quality references
9.00	**Extensibility**
9.01	Provides a data model (metamodel) for metadata managed by tool
9.02	Provides tool metamodel which is extensible and can be customized
9.03	Provides nonproprietary tool metamodel
9.04	Provides interfaces with existing tools and systems through robust and customizable APIs and connectors
9.05	Permits the customer to add to the metadata captured and managed by identifying and collecting new (previously not identified metadata)
9.06	Permits metadata extensions as attributes (e.g., supports open standards)
9.07	Permits metadata extensions as entities (e.g., supports open standards)
9.08	Supports custom code extensions that manage the added attributes and entities
9.09	Provides APIs so that client applications may use the metadata to direct processing
9.10	Allows for both data coming into the catalog and data going out through APIs

#	Feature
9.11	Provides an extensive API library and the ability to create customized APIs
10.00	**Metadata Attributes**
10.01	Provides basic descriptive attributes including name, description, size such as number of rows and number of columns
10.02	Provides documented and inferred data type, such as string, integer, and date
10.03	Supports multiple data formats, such as relational, JSON, XML, and Microsoft Office documents
10.04	Provides the location of the data set
10.05	Captures the submitter of a data set (see POC's above)
10.06	Supports the ability to collect records management attributes
10.07	Captures data set creation date, last update date, metadata collection date, and last refresh date
10.08	Provides number of rows in the table and other size attributes
10.09	Defines data type and inferred data type for database columns
10.10	Supports the ability to include a schema for informing parsing (see format specifications above)
10.11	Displays users (and top users) of a data set
10.12	Displays a Data Usage Agreement (DUA) for a data asset
10.13	Displays data stewards, Subject Matter Experts (SMEs), stakeholders and top users for a data set
10.14	Displays business domains related to a data asset
10.15	Displays sample data
10.16	Displays descriptive statistics/data profiling results (see Data Profiling section)
10.17	Displays related tags
10.18	Displays the governed status of an asset if applicable

#	Feature
10.19	Displays related data assets
10.20	Recommends data assets based on your search behavior or that of others
11.00	**Data Governance, Privacy and Risk**
11.01	Provides certification, warnings, and deprecation of data sets
11.02	Uses icons to identify assets as certified, warnings, or privacy
11.03	Supports management of data set POCs (i.e., source, contributor, stewards, subject matter experts, and curators)
11.04	Provides the definition and amendment of data governance workflows
11.05	Supports data access requests, Shopping Cart for data, and access approval workflow
11.06	Provides automatic notification of requests/orders placed by users
11.07	Provides the ability to visually map, update, and automate process workflow steps
11.08	Implements role-based governance in the workflows
11.09	Provide different access and governance roles including a rich collection out of the box and the ability to customize and add roles
11.10	Supports protected data classes/tags (i.e. PII), both out-of-the-box and creation of custom classes
11.11	Includes customizable rules for handling of sensitive data types/classes
11.12	Masks sensitive data as a native feature of the catalog
11.13	Creates (and stores) a hash of the data
11.14	Hides sample data for sensitive categories
11.15	Configures the blocking of sensitive data display in asset pages and profiling

#	Feature
11.16	Provides policy governance (creation of a policy as a governable asset)
11.17	Creates rules tied to policies
11.18	Edits rules to adjust the level of governance on an asset
11.19	Ties physical data to rules and policies, such as traceability of data that is governed and/or protected by a policy
11.20	Manages risk through display of risk dashboard
11.21	Manages replication by auto detection of potential duplicates
11.22	Provides the ability for owners to view all of the entries they "own"
11.23	Captures the status of governed attributes, such as pending, approved, and submitted
11.24	Creates warnings for potentially incorrect data usage
11.25	Provides security around roles that can edit
12.00	**Business Glossary**
12.01	Offers hierarchical business glossary structure for multiple glossaries and sub-glossaries
12.02	Allows glossary terms to be developed, governed, and managed like any other data asset (i.e., approval workflow)
12.03	Displays the status of a term, including candidate, pending, and approved
12.04	Identifies synonyms
12.05	Controls vocabulary and taxonomy development or integration
12.06	Provides related and preferred terms, "is a," "has a" relationships
12.07	Provides acronyms and abbreviations as attributes of a business term
12.08	Associates terms with all other assets including technical metadata, business domains, and business processes
12.09	Associates glossaries (sets of terms) with organizations/divisions that have jurisdiction over the glossary

#	Feature
12.10	Displays the data steward/owner of each term and/or glossary
13.00	**Data Quality**
13.01	Supports development and enforcement of data quality policies for catalog entries/fields
13.02	Creates data quality rules, computes data quality metrics based upon rules
13.03	Creates thresholds for data quality rules and actively report assets that are out of bounds of thresholds
13.04	Displays data quality level/metrics in asset pages
13.05	Customizes data quality metrics algorithm or weights
13.06	Notifies of quality failures via workflow and/or subscribed notifications
13.07	Displays data quality dashboard
13.08	Supports algorithms that expose data conflicts or identify data deficiencies
14.00	**Data Profiling**
14.01	Provides data profiling of entire data set (not just a sample)
14.02	Includes data profiling of all the basic statistics, including min, max. # of rows, #/% null, #/% distinct, for number fields mean, average, value frequency distribution
14.03	Support data profiling of pattern frequency distribution
14.04	Offers interactive data profiling (or the ability to drill into lower grains, in other words drill to underlying data from a profile, for a max or min value, see the other data in the row)
14.05	Offers the ability to turn off data profiling on a data set (such as sensitive data restrictions)
14.06	Presents data profiling in an easy-to-understand format, included in or accessible from the main asset page

#	Feature
14.07	Provides the ability to tune how often profile statistics are run
14.08	Masks or hides sensitive data in profiles
14.09	Displays the date/time when the last statistics were run
14.10	Provides data profiling on data other than relational such as JSON or XML
15.00	**Data Lineage**
15.01	Captures and infers lineage/provenance of technical data flow
15.02	Ties business asset (such as business process, business purpose) to technical data
15.03	Associates business glossary to technical: manual
15.04	Associates business glossary to technical: inferred by ML
15.05	Uses a diagram for presentation of data lineage
15.06	Provides warnings for broken lineage
15.07	Enables drill down into lower levels of data lineage/more granular details
15.08	Provides an API for ingest of data for lineage purposes that is not in the native connectors of the tool
15.09	Provides the ability to drill down to the transformation level of an ETL job
15.10	Provides lineage through partner relationships with 3rd party data integration vendors
16.00	**Architecture/Administration/Infrastructure/Security**
16.01	Offers role-based, group, and individual access control and access rights
16.02	Supports the collection and application of access control attributes (classification, such as Secret, Top Secret)
16.03	Provides security control over roles that have edit privileges

#	Feature
16.04	Scales, meaning able to support large amounts of data, large data sets and large number of concurrent users
16.05	Filters and captures database schemas upon ingest
16.06	Separates roles between data management functions
16.07	Supports existing security infrastructure and processes for user authentication and authorization (i.e. LDAP)
16.08	Supports a federated view across complex environments, catalog agents or a "catalog of catalogs"
16.09	Provides an archival capability for assets
16.10	Provides an auditing of catalog activity
16.11	Provides catalog activity metrics
16.12	Includes administration notifications and alerts
16.13	Provides usage reporting of data assets, including most used and least used
16.14	Connects to all required types of data sets and all system/platform infrastructure in the enterprise ecosystem
16.15	Offers their solution as a service on a vendor cloud
16.16	Offers their solution on a commercial cloud - federal government approval
16.17	Works across hybrid cloud architecture and on-premise
17.00	**Data Prep**
17.01	Offers a data prep facility built into the catalog
17.02	Offers a query builder functionality for non-technical users
17.03	Recommends data sets that can be joined with the viewed data set both based on defined PK/FK constraints and inferred relationships
17.04	Offers a job launcher and scheduler
17.05	Offers job status and logging

#	Feature
17.06	Provides a reuse of functions/filters for data sets that have already been defined for a given data set
17.07	Provides the ability to clone/reuse a query
18.00	**Business Domains and Processes**
18.01	Supports business processes and tying them to physical assets
18.02	Supports business domains and tying them to physical assets
19.00	**Data Analyst Tool/Big Data Integration**
19.01	Provides ability to integrate with data scientist or reporting tool metadata
19.02	Provides the ability to integrate with other data catalogs to create an Enterprise Catalog (architecture)
19.03	Integrates/launches data scientist analysis workbench and AI tools such as R Studio within the catalog
19.04	Handles large volume auto metadata ingest with complex data at scale

Scoring

You can use this feature list for soliciting ratings from staff. If you do, be aware that some features are qualitative and subjectively determined (like friendliness of GUI) and some are binary, such as does the product have this feature (Y/N)? Some involve rating the degree that it has that feature, such as support for data access requests.

You can build your own product assessment tool in Excel. For example, you can assign weights to features to reflect the degree of importance they have to your organization. You can create a sheet for every reviewer. Each sheet will multiply the score given to the feature by the weighting, and the master sheet will aggregate all the scores from each reviewer for each feature and provide an average. Then all the combined aggregated scores can be tallied for each feature category. Figure 11-1 shows a screenshot from a tool that The MITRE Corporation created called CAATS for alternatives comparison which shows three alternatives compared.

Figure 11-1. CAATS feature comparison

Key points

This chapter provided an extensive features list for data catalogs, organized by category. Most of these features have been covered in the body of the book. The features list can be very beneficial in determining what is important for your organization. You can access this as an Excel workbook on our book's web page at https://technicspub.com/TheDataCatalog/. We hope it will be helpful.

## CHAPTER 12

Conclusion

The power of deduction

This book has told the Data Catalog story. A data catalog provides much more than just a data inventory: it's a central place for data management and a launching pad for data analytics. It serves as a personal detective for the analyst and data scientist, guiding them on the quest to figure out what data they need, where it came from, which data can be trusted, what cleanup is necessary and what data sets can potentially be linked for enrichment. It offloads much of the pre-investigative grunt work that the analyst must do before the study can be conducted, freeing them up for the fun part, which is performing the statistical modeling and analytics. It saves them a large amount of time, and perhaps saves them even more aggravation.

We call the data catalog functionality "Sherlock Holmes Data Sleuthing for Analytics" because it can use ML brainpower, deduction, and inferences to produce new knowledge for the researcher to launch their study. Sherlock Holmes was famous for his incredible gift of deduction. Wikipedia defines *deduction* as *"... inference deriving logical conclusions from premises known or assumed to be true."*[38]

We cannot resist the urge to quote from the great mastermind behind Sherlock Holmes, Sir Arthur Conan Doyle. The interesting, little known fact about Sherlock Holmes is he did not consider himself as the greatest bearer of the gift

---

[38]https://en.wikipedia.org/wiki/Inference (August 6.2019).

of observation and deduction. He says, "…my brother Mycroft possesses it in a larger degree than I do."[39] But Mycroft could not use his gift—he possessed no ambition and no energy. Together, however, their gifts of observation and deduction were unparalleled. Here's a quote from "The Greek Interpreter" showcasing their amazing skills:

"The two sat down together in the bow-window of the club. "To anyone who wishes to study mankind this is the spot," said Mycroft. "Look at the magnificent types! Look at these two men who are coming towards us, for example." "The billiard-marker and the other?" "Precisely. What do you make of the other?"

The two men had stopped opposite the window. Some chalk marks over the waistcoat pocket were the only signs of billiards which I could see in one of them. The other was a very small, dark fellow, with his hat pushed back and several packages under his arm.

"An old soldier, I perceive," said Sherlock. "And very recently discharged," remarked the brother.

"Served in India, I see." "And a non-commissioned officer." "Royal Artillery, I fancy," said Sherlock.

"And a widower." "But with a child."

"Children, my dear boy, children."

"Come," said I, laughing, "this is a little too much." "Surely," answered Holmes, "it is not hard to say that a man with that bearing, expression of authority, and sunbaked skin, is a soldier, is more than a private, and is not long from India." "That he has not left the service long is shown by his still wearing his 'ammunition boots', as they are called," observed Mycroft. "He had not the cavalry stride, yet he wore his hat on one side, as is shown by the lighter skin of that side of his brow. His weight is against his

---

[39] Sir Arthur Conan Doyle, "The Greek Interpreter." https://bit.ly/2tXYPtS.

being a sapper. He is in the artillery." "Then, of course, his complete mourning shows that he has lost someone very dear. The fact that he is doing his own shopping looks as though it were his wife. He has been buying things for children, you perceive. There is a rattle, which shows that one of them is very young. The wife probably died in childbed. The fact that he has a picture-book under his arm shows that there is another child to be thought of." I began to understand what my friend meant when he said that his brother possessed even keener faculties that he did himself."[40]

This excerpt showcases the observations that most may miss, and how the set of observations can be masterfully joined to arrive at the conclusion. Sherlock Holmes uses this method of observation and deduction in service to Scotland Yard to take the conclusions he weaves together and solve many cases that elude the police.

We cannot call the book, "Mycroft Holmes Data Sleuthing," because no one knows who Mycroft Holmes is. The moral of the story here is it takes more than just the mechanics—it is the ability to use the skills to accomplish great things. Mycroft was lazy. Sherlock had motivation, determination, and energy. Data catalogs must be able to leverage ML and AI in skillful ways to provide the "back story" behind the data, so that the analyst can piece together the facts presented in order to conduct their research. The data catalog must provide the power of both the great mind and the ingenuity to use it to empower data analytics and business insight.

We have explained the data catalog by bringing some of the main vendors to center stage, letting them tell the story and weaving in commentary to clarify and enhance the narrative. We have introduced the need for data catalogs, and why they are necessary in today's data glut world. We have illustrated this need by telling the contrasting stories of two fictitious data scientists, one dealing

---

[40] Ibid.

with the frustrations of trying to find data without a data catalog and one fortunate to benefit from the data catalog.

We have illustrated the user-friendly features and how they help by second guessing what the user is going to enter, and so helping the search go faster and smarter. We have shown how catalogs can help both technical and non-technical users alike construct queries faster.

Data catalogs must have governance and curation as their backbone. ML relies on humans to provide the feedback concerning the veracity of its inferences. Our data governance chapter reinforced the importance of governance and demonstrated how the data catalog can enable data governance, which is the mainstay of data management.

Data lakes have potential to be repositories for the vast quantities of data flooding the enterprise but they can also quickly become "swamps" if there's no metadata to provide an understanding of their contents. Data catalogs are just the thing to be able to add context and meaning to the data lake. They are therefore a necessary component. Chapter 6 provided an illustration of how data catalogs can provide this index into the contents of the lake, allowing the analyst to productively "fish" for their data.

The data catalog provides the ability to be an integrated data management resource for all data citizens, including data stewards, data quality engineers, and administrators as well as data scientists. The "one-stop shop" data catalog provides an integrated platform for all data management activities, which not only helps those users providing these services, it gives all users a window into the status and quality of data that they are considering for their study. Chapter 7 illustrated two products that are examples of this and are perfect candidates for an enterprise data catalog.

We briefly discussed products that have provided data catalog add-on capability on top of their tools other functionality. Cataloging is an extremely useful functionality and can enhance many different offerings. Most data-oriented tools capture and generate metadata which can be harvested and used in a catalog to help users find and use data more effectively.

One of the most important features of data catalogs is their ability to trace the provenance of data and provide lineage of all different types. Regulations require that the purpose of certain categories of data be tracked along with its source. Data scientists often need to know where the data came from to determine if it is trustworthy. Data usage agreements need to be tied to the data they govern. Business terms need to be associated with the technical data they explain so the data can be understood. Data lineage is therefore very important. We show examples of all these different types of lineage and the diagrams that illustrate it. This is an emerging trend in catalogs, and vendors are working hard at increasing their ability to ingest and exploit more types of lineage from a wider variety of sources.

ML is the "secret sauce" that makes data catalogs so powerful. A catalog product that is not ML-augmented simply will not be able to handle the vast array of data volume and complexity. We illustrated why this is true and peeled back the covers to demonstrate what ML provides and how it enables the inferences made from associating many different types of data assets. It is these connections that provide the analyst with knowledge and insight to choose the right data to use.

We concluded the adventure with an exhaustive features list organized by category. The reader can get a feel for the vast array of functionality that data catalogs can offer by scanning the 19 categories and almost 200 different features listed. It is no wonder that many prospective buyers are overwhelmed with the prospect of trying to make sense of these products in order to make a choice. It is hoped that this book will help you in your journey of understanding the benefits of these powerful products and help to determine which capabilities are necessary for your use cases.

Trends and innovations

Data catalog products are maturing rapidly. Many vendors are using Agile methodologies and releasing new features at a very fast rate, some as quickly as 6-8 weeks. The need is fueling up, as the Federal Government's Foundations for Evidence-Based Policymaking Act mandates that all Federal Agencies establish a data inventory, which can only realistically be met by a data catalog. It is, therefore, a race to see which vendors can offer more and more sophisticated technology that is easy to use, enabling data democratization and faster to insight.

Data lineage

One of the fastest areas of growth in the catalog capabilities is data lineage. Catalog vendors are investing heavily in both partnerships and in-house development to strengthen the breadth and depth of their data lineage. Several vendors mentioned that they are creating strategic partnerships with vendors that specialize in lineage. Lineage is a complex area because it involves not only metadata ingest but the ability to stitch it together and make connections with other metadata. This is why the vendors are working hard to innovate in this area.

GUI

Another area of innovation is the look and feel of the Graphical User Interface (GUI). This particular push is fueled by the anticipated growth, maturation, and sophistication of users. 451 Research states that:

> *Data engineers are currently the primary users of data catalogs, but in the next two years primary usage is expected to shift toward data executives (chief data officers, chief analytics officers, etc.)[41]*

Figure 12-1 shows the results of 451's research study concerning the number of users in each role category both currently (the study was conducted in October 2018) and in the next two years. This means that it is more important that business users be comfortable with the data catalog, and it should be businessperson friendly.

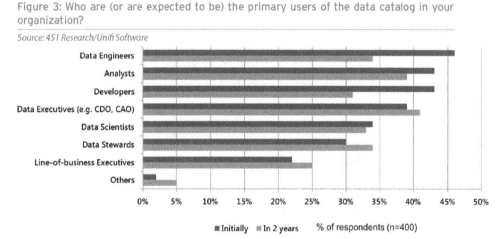

Figure 3: Who are (or are expected to be) the primary users of the data catalog in your organization?

Source: 451 Research/Unifi Software

Figure 12-1. Primary user roles of the data catalog[42]

---

[41] Aslett, Matt. "From Out of Nowhere: the Unstoppable Rise of the Data Catalog", 451 Research, October 10, 2018.

Integration with data management capabilities

Even tools that offer strong data management integration are beefing up their offerings in these disciplines. Both IBM and Informatica are leaders in this area, and both are bringing more functionality to bear from even stronger alignment with their data management tools. Some products offer solid reference data management already in the catalog and are slowly phasing in more Master Data Management functions. The trajectory is towards being able to launch the capability directly from the catalog and have the results visible to users as required. This means being able to see survivor rules and the results of mastering and merging master records from the catalog. The goal is for the catalog to be the launching pad for all data management and governance functions. This will not only help data stewards and data owners but citizen users, who can benefit by seeing a 360-degree view of data including lineage, data quality, reference and master data, as their permissions allow.

ML

ML is an obvious growth area. More research is going into creating smarter algorithms to improve the inference capabilities of the catalog.

APIs, extensibility and partnerships

Several vendors reported that they are working with other vendors to create complementary technology. For example, vendors that do not offer data profiling are partnering with data profiling specialty vendors. This is easy for some of the vendors that already provide extensible APIs. It will be exciting to

---

[42] Ibid.

watch as these alliances come to fruition. This is especially true in the area of data lineage, as mentioned above.

Vendors are also working on their APIs and adding more, so their catalogs will be more extensible. This gives organizations the ability to customize the catalog for themselves, linking it to other tools both as inbound and outbound. This means catalog metadata can be fed to other tools such as prep/data wrangling and data science workbenches as well as other tools feeding their metadata to populate the catalog, such as the data profiling example mentioned above.

Where would we like them to go?

Standards

There have been several attempts at metadata standards in the past, and new ones are emerging. The Dublin Core Metadata Initiative was established over 20 years ago and curates the Dublin Core Specifications, which is a list of metadata terms that describe both digital and physical resources. It is an ISO (International Standards Organization) standard. Meta Integration Technology Inc. (MITI) has created metadata bridges that enable tools to share metadata. The Digital Curation Centre (DCC) is an international organization, "…with a focus on building capability and skills for research data management." They maintain a list of metadata standards.[43]

The data catalog will continue to mature, and with it, we hope that a data catalog metadata standard will emerge. APIs are wonderful and provide a means to extend a specific data catalog product, but they resemble the point-to-

---

[43] http://www.dcc.ac.uk/resources/metadata-standards/list.

point interfaces of data warehouse from yesteryear. These interfaces linked a specific data source to a specific target. The more sources were brought in, the more the number of interfaces proliferated. APIs are similar—there's an API for a single source to a specific catalog product. When the catalog comes out with a new version that changes its underlying metadata, you hope there will be a migration path for all of the APIs you created with the last version. The concern goes in the other direction perhaps with even more difficulty, managing all the changes from the many connected tools. It becomes a change and configuration management overhead, requiring additional resources to keep up. This will not be acceptable in the self-service world of the future.

A better approach would be a standard that would cover all the metadata classes that the catalogs support—and there's a lot of them, both business and technical. We hope that such a standard will emerge in the near future, and that all the vendors will support it. This will enable siloed data catalogs to be linked with the enterprise without concern about different proprietary products. This would also enable data catalogs to interface with other catalogs, leveraging any investments the organization might have in siloed catalogs and making the vision of an enterprise data catalog possible. However, there exists the need to put a fence around a data catalog that contains privacy data, classified, or requires special usage agreements and protection. This data must not be discoverable by non-privileged users.

Industry templates

There are different types of metadata such as that which support the financial, medical, and insurance industries, to name a few. We can see a potential need for data catalog templates to support these industries. The catalog would be able to offer "out of the box" support to many types of metadata such as glossary terms, business policies, and regulations common to the industry, eliminating the need for organizations to have to set up this metadata manually. This would help a great deal in onboarding the data catalog for these industries, which will be big users of data catalogs in the near term.

Communities of Practice can also be formed to support these industries, and "birds of a feather" catalog user groups can facilitate adoption and efficient usage.

Catalog as a Service

The "as a service" concept means that the product offered by the technology is provided on demand, regardless of platform. IBM provided its business glossary as "Glossary Anywhere," and Collibra had its "Glossary Everywhere," allowing you to launch the glossary anywhere, no matter what application you are in. We see the data catalog in the future as being a "catalog anywhere," "catalog as a service." No matter what application you are in, you can invoke the catalog and get the results of a search on demand.

Another example of catalog as a service can be seen in usage of a statistical tool such as SAS. The user discovers a glossary term or potential tag, and then the user would highlight the object or term and invoke the catalog to ingest the term or tag.

Personal catalog

Suppose you had your own data catalog? You can use it to find the report you produced last year because you don't remember where you stored it. Is it on your PC? A SharePoint? Perhaps the only copy you have is an attachment to an email. The catalog can find it.

Perhaps you could use it for broader applications: I (Bonnie) love to go to the opera. I don't buy my opera tickets online, because I'm a season ticket holder, so Google (or a catalog) doesn't know that I like opera. The catalog would need to know that I like opera. If it did, when I'm booking travel to see my family in Florida, it could suggest "would you like to see an opera when you are in Tampa? 'Aida' is playing at Opera Tampa when you will be there." Perhaps it would know that I like opera from my playlists in Napster! Songs in playlists are data assets. This concept extends the notion of internet search (and advertisements) to a new level. It uses an inventory and index of files and data assets, coupled with a recommender engine for preferences. Right now, I'm too busy to look up operas that might be available in my destination venue. However, this is a recommendation that I would welcome, and it would enrich my life experience. This is an example of an advertisement that I would look at and would not be an annoyance!

Data ethics and responsible AI

The more you use the catalog, the smarter it gets for you, but perhaps "Big Brother" knows more than you want, bringing up the criticality of privacy concerns.

Therefore, another potential data catalog application would be assisting the use of AI and protecting the user from its unethical use. The data catalog can display warnings when the data scientist is using data in a statistical model or AI work that may be violating an ethics policy. The DAMA DMBOK2 has a chapter on data ethics.

The data catalog can enforce preferences in the external sharing of personal data. In the example above, I don't think I want Google or other external entities to know of my personal life, so I want to set up a data-sharing policy that allows the catalog to perform affinity analysis and recommendations but not share this knowledge with other external entities such as Facebook or Google. The catalog can crawl external sources to discover where my data is located in applications and databases online. This enables me to use the catalog to request the removal of my data in those locations that are undesirable ("forget me").

Data diaries and analysis breadcrumbs

Another future application of the data catalog involves the creative use of analysis history. Experian's Pandora data profiling tool has a feature that I call "breadcrumbs" (my name, not theirs!). The user explores data using the data profiling tool, which is more robust than just profiling, as it allows you to apply filters on the data and then profile again, and apply more filters and profile again. It remembers which filters you applied, then you can press a button and ETL code or instructions are created consisting of every step you made.

We can see the data catalog performing this function in the future, remembering your hypotheses so that you can retrace your steps and refine your analysis to obtain your desired outcome. It remembers the context of what you've done including what you haven't done. You may even want to annotate the analysis process to explain why you chose one path over another. Sometimes what you didn't do becomes almost as important as what you did. For example, online retailers monitor users' responses to ads and offers. They learn just as much from which offers were not taken as from which ones were. They learn that one type of user doesn't respond to sale announcements but does take the offer of free shipping, for example. Apply this technique to data analysis: The user can trace the steps of the analysis and make an observation like, "THAT'S why I didn't choose that path because ___."

Administration

Data catalogs can act as a digital thermometer, continuously taking the temperature of data. It can monitor factors like:

- Recent/stale
- Access frequency
- Usefulness

The catalog can then make recommendations to the administrator concerning the treatment of this data, such as:

- Choice of processing
- Compute resources/memory
- Storage
- Cloud migration

The catalog can warn users that they are browsing data that may be stale, or data that hasn't been used in a while.

Key points

The data catalog can empower and establish a new goal for the Chief Data Officer, which is building an organization of insights. The data catalog, with its ML insight affinity, can provide true data self-service to all data citizens at scale, and help them to achieve the vision of data democratization. 451 Research begins its paper on the "Unstoppable Rise of the data catalog" with the following:

Could the data catalog be the most important data management breakthrough to have emerged in the last decade? There's certainly a case to be made given its importance in enabling modern analytics architecture.[44]

We agree. The data catalog is the most important breakthrough in data management in the last decade, and maybe even rivals the advent of the data warehouse. The latter took the back office statistical scientist capabilities into the front office, enabling business consumers to conduct their own analyses to obtain their own insights. The data catalog is the next wave, enabling business users even more reduced time to insight, despite the rising tide of data flooding the enterprise. Sherlock Holmes was able to quickly deduce insights from sharp observations and make brilliant connections. The data catalog does this too. Powerful indeed, and an enormous breakthrough.

---

[44] Use https://clients.451research.com/reportaction/95778/Toc? Figure ©451 Research, used by permission.

Glossary

Term or Acronym	Definition
ADS	Authoritative Data Source: a data set that is deemed "official" or "certified."
Aggregate	A summary function such as AVERAGE or SUM.
AI	Artificial Intelligence: The theory and development of computer systems able to perform tasks normally requiring human intelligence, such as visual perception, speech recognition, decision-making, and translation between languages.[45]
API	Application Programming Interface: the ability to share data to and from a software application.
Asset	An *asset* is a highly valuable resource which merits management. Assets include money, real estate and personnel, all of which contribute to the organization's ability to perform its mission.
BI	Business Intelligence: reporting and analysis intended to improve business decision-making.
Big Data	Extremely large data sets that may be analyzed computationally to reveal patterns, trends, and associations, especially related to human behavior and interactions.
Business Glossary	A data repository containing business terminology, organized into categories and hierarchies. Can be expressed as a taxonomy, controlled vocabulary, or ontology. It is the language of the business.
Business Metadata	Business metadata is metadata that focuses on the business use of the data and supplies the context of the data.
Crawling	The automated process of systematically navigating through a file system or other storage area for the purpose of data ingest.

---

[45] https://www.lexico.com/en/definition/artificial_intelligence.

Term or Acronym	Definition
Crowdsourcing	The ability to allow users to collaborate concerning data assets, to comment, rate , ask questions, and discuss problems.
Curation	The partnership of human interaction with a ML-augmented data catalog to make sense of, properly manage, and protect data.
Curator	A person who is involved with the custodianship of the data catalog. Can be an administrator or data steward.
Dark Data	Data in the enterprise that is not documented and hard to find.
Dashboard	A visual display of KPIs and charts depicting the status of the business.
Data Asset	The realization that data is a valuable resource which has great potential to help the organization to realize its mission, and as such merits special management and governance.
Data Catalog	A data catalog is an inventory of data assets that enables users to discover and explore all the data sources available, enhancing their understanding of these sources, and enabling collaboration with other users to enrich the quality of the assets and to achieve more value from the organization's data.
Data Certification	A designation publishing the fact to all users that the quality of a data asset is sufficiently acceptable.
Data Dictionary	A list of data elements and definitions, sometimes also includes other descriptive metadata such as data type, length, mandatory/optional.
Data Governance	Data governance is the discipline of administering data and information assets across an organization through formal oversight of the people, processes, technologies and lines of business that influence data and information outcomes to drive business performance.
Data Lake	A repository of raw data.

Term or Acronym	Definition
Data Lineage	The tracing of data flow, which can include source to target systems and applications, business terms to physical data assets, rules, and business purposes. Usually represented by a diagram.
Data Mart	A specialized data structure used to enable BI reporting.
Data Prep	Data Preparation: the process of preparing the data for fitness for use. See Data Wrangling.
Data profiling	Descriptive statistics about a table or other data asset including minimum, maximum values in a column, number of nulls, and patterns.
Data Quality	The assessment of a data asset's fitness of purpose.
Data Scientist	A person employed to analyze and interpret complex digital data, such as the usage statistics of a website, especially in order to assist a business in its decision-making.
Data Self-Service	The ability to allow users to search for, prepare, and use data on their own without the assistance of IT staff.
Data Steward	A role assigned to an individual to govern a data asset.
Data Virtualization	Integrates data from diverse sources in memory.
Data Visualization	A class of tools that creates charts, graphs, and dashboards showing status of KPIs.
Data Warehouse	A central repository of data usually sourced from different systems integrated and modeled to enable reporting.
Data Wrangling	Sometimes referred to as data munging, it is the process of transforming and mapping data from one "raw" data form into another format with the intent of making it more appropriate and valuable for a variety of downstream purposes such as analytics.[46]
DDL	Data Definition Language: the commands in SQL that define data structures in a relational database.

---

[46] https://en.wikipedia.org/wiki/Data_wrangling.

Term or Acronym	Definition
Deprecation	A designation that the data set will be archived or going away.
ELT	Extract, Load then Transform.
Enterprise Data	Data that is used in more than one business area in the organization and is usually deemed as important to the business.
Enterprise Data Catalog	A data catalog that enables searches that span silos, bridging these silos and making data all over the enterprise discoverable.
ETL	Extract, Transform, and Load.
Folksonomy	Folksonomy is the process of using digital content tags for categorization or annotation. It allows users to classify websites, pictures, documents, and other forms of data so that content may be easily categorized and located by users. Folksonomy is also known as social tagging, collaborative tagging, social classification, and social bookmarking.[47]
Foundations for Evidence-Based Policymaking Act of 2018	A law stating that Federal Agencies comply with specific policies regarding the traceability of data assets. It mandates the establishment of a Chief Data Officer and a data inventory, among others.
GUI	Graphical User Interface.
Histogram	A visual representation of the value distribution in a column of data.
Ingest	The importing of metadata from data sources.
IoT	Internet of Things.
JSON	Java Script Object Notation.

---

[47] https://www.techopedia.com/definition/30196/folksonomy.

Term or Acronym	Definition
Knowledge Graph	A programmatic way to model a knowledge domain with the help of subject-matter experts, data interlinking, and machine learning algorithms.[48]
KPI	Key Performance Indicator: how business measures its performance in major areas.
Machine Learning	An application of Artificial Intelligence (AI) that provides systems the ability to automatically learn and improve from experience without being explicitly programmed.[49]
Mask	To hide data from view when it is protected and the user does not have access.
Master Data	Represents the business concepts that contain the most valuable, agreed upon information shared across an organization.
MDM	Master Data Management.
Metadata	Data that describes other data, adding context to the data.
Metric	A measure that the business uses to gauge its performance. An example of a class of metric is KPI.
Null	A value used in a database column to represent the fact that data in the column is "unknown" or not applicable in some way. It is not the same thing as an empty field but may have a similar meaning. Summaries often cannot be performed properly if nulls exist, and the developer usually must convert them to zero or to another value to perform the summary.
Overloading	Use of a field for a purpose other than that which it was originally designed.
PHI	Personal Health Information.
PII	Personally Identifiable Information.

---

[48]https://bit.ly/38OSb82.

[49] https://www.expertsystems.com/.

Term or Acronym	Definition
Portal	A publishing platform for data content.
Primary Key	Used in relational database tables to join one principle table to a secondary, detail table. For example an Order ID would be the Primary Key in an Order Header table and would appear in a detail table such as Order Details, which would allow the detail rows such as the products purchased to be associated with the date of the order.
Query Log	A log of all queries conducted on a data set(s) within a tool.
Reference Data	Used to organize or categorize other data. Often reference data includes code sets that serve as shorthand for longer named elements.
Similarity	The process of discovering and presenting assets that are alike and could potentially be duplicates.
SME	Subject Matter Expert: a business person who specializes in a business subject area and can offer advice on data in that subject area. Usually refers to an informal role.
SOR	Source of Record, the point at which data is created or imported, that is, the point of origin.
Tag	An informal classification that can be created by users to assign to data assets to assist with search.
Technical Metadata	That data generated by IT products tracing all the technical information about the data.

References

"7 Modern Data Projects that Demand Interactive Data Profiling," Paxata, Redwood City, CA, 2017.

"AI-Powered Data Cataloging and Governance for Evidence-Based Policymaking Act," Informatica, Redwood City, CA. 2019.

"Consuming Data Productively: The Five Ways a Data Catalog Drives Productive Self-Service Analytics." Alation, Redwood City, CA.

"DAMA-DMBOK: Data Management Body of Knowledge." 2nd Edition. Technics Publications. Basking Ridge, NJ.

"Data Catalog: Creating a Single Source of Reference," Alation, Redwood City, CA.

"Enterprise Data Catalog Use Cases," Unifi Software, San Mateo, CA. 2019.

"Gartner Peer Insights 'Voice of the Customer': Data Preparation Tools," Gartner Group, Stamford, CT, Rep ID G00402992, 2019.

Aslett, M. "From Out of Nowhere: The Unstoppable Rise of the Data Catalog," 451 Research, New York, NY, 2018.

De Simoni, G. "Metadata is the Fish Finder in Data Lakes," Gartner Group, Stamford, CT, Rep ID G00274543, 2015.

De Simoni, G., Beyer, M. and Jain, A. "Gartner Magic Quadrant for Metadata Management Solutions," Gartner Group, Stamford, CT, Rep ID G00372820, 2019.

Dresner, H. and Hostmann, B. "Data Catalog Study, Wisdom of Crowds Series," Dresner Advisory Services, Nashua, NH, 2019.

Duncan, A.D., Zaidi, E., DeSimoni, G. and La ney, D. "Applied Infonomics: Use a Modern Data Catalog to Measure, Manage, and Monitize Information Supply Chains." Gartner Group, Stamford, CT. Rep ID G00342785, 2018.

Fadzeyeva, F. and Cavallaro, R. "The Total Economic Impact of the Alation Data Catalog," Forrester Research, Cambridge, MA, 2019.

Goetz, M. "Now Tech: Machine Learning Data Catalogs, Q1 2018," Forrester Research, Cambridge, MA, 2018.

Goetz, M. "Reclaim Your Semantic Desert To Monetize Your Data," Gartner Group, Stamford, CT, Rep ID G00372820, 2018.

Goetz, M. "The Forrester Wave: Machine Learning Data Catalogs, Q2 2018," Forrester Research, Cambridge, MA, 2018.

Gorelik, A. The Enterprise Big Data Lake: Delivering the Promise of Big Data and Data Science." Sebastopol, CA: O'Reilly Media, Inc. 2019.

Halper, F."Five Benefits of Modern Data Catalogs," TDWI, Renton, WA, 2018.

Henschen, D. "How to Blend Self-Service and Solid Governance for the Hybrid Data Lake: Balance Accessibility and Control across Cloud and On-Premises Big Data Deployments," Constellation Research, CA. 2018.

Heudecker, N and Ronthal, A. "How to Avoid Data Lake Failures," Gartner Group, Stamford, CT. Rep ID G00367848, 2018.

Pal, S. "Building Data Lakes Successfully," Gartner Group, Stamford, CT, Rep ID G00378068, 2019.

Perret, R. "From Data to Disruption: Innovation Through Digital Intelligence," Harvard Business Review Analytic Services Report, Boston, MA. 2016.

Pike, S and Marden, M. "Quantifying the Business Value of the Collibra Data Governance and Data Platform," IDC, Framingham, MA. #US43978718, 2018.

Unifi Data Platform User's Guide, v3.0, Unifi Software, San Mateo, CA. 2018.

Wells, D. "The Business Value of a Data Catalog," Eckerson Group, Hingham, MA, 2019.

Wells, D. "The Ultimate Guide to Data Catalogs: Key Things to Consider When Selecting a Data Catalog," Eckerson Group, Hingham, MA, 2018.

Zaidi, E., De Simoni, G. "Augmented Data Catalogs: Now an Enterprise Must-Have for Data and Analytics Leaders," Gartner Group, Stamford, CT, Rep ID G00394570, 2017.

Zaidi, E., De Simoni, G., Edjlali, R and Duncan, A.D. "Data Catalogs are the New Black in Data Management and Analytics," Gartner Group, Stamford, CT, Rep ID G00338777, 2017.

Index

www.ingramcontent.com/pod-product-compliance
Lightning Source LLC
Chambersburg PA
CBHW080630060326

40690CB00021B/4879